THE UPPER ROOM

YOUR PLACE TO MEET GOD

Sarah Wilke
Publisher

Lynne M. Deming
World Editor

INTERDENOMINATIONAL
INTERNATIONAL
INTERRACIAL

77 EDITIONS
35 LANGUAGES

The Upper Room
May–August 2013
Edited by Susan Hibbins

The Upper Room © BRF 2013
The Bible Reading Fellowship
15 The Chambers, Vineyard, Abingdon OX14 3FE
Tel: 01865 319700; Fax: 01865 319701
Email: enquiries@brf.org.uk
Website: www.brf.org.uk
BRF is a Registered Charity

ISBN 978 0 85746 109 4

Acknowledgments

The New Revised Standard Version of the Bible, Anglicised Edition, copyright © 1989, 1995 by the Division of Christian Education of the National Council of the Churches of Christ in the USA. Used by permission. All rights reserved.

The Holy Bible, New International Version (Anglicised edition), copyright © 1978, 1984, 2011 by Biblica (formerly International Bible Society). Used by permission of Hodder & Stoughton Publishers, an Hachette UK company. All rights reserved. 'NIV' is a registered trademark of Biblica (formerly International Bible Society). UK trademark number 1448790.

Extracts from the Authorised Version of the Bible (The King James Bible), the rights in which are vested in the Crown, are reproduced by permission of the Crown's Patentee, Cambridge University Press.

Extracts from CEB copyright © 2011 by Common English Bible.

Printed in the UK by MWL.

The Upper Room is ideal in helping us spend a quiet time with God each day. Each daily entry is based on a passage of scripture, and is followed by a meditation and prayer. Each person who contributes a meditation to the magazine seeks to relate their experience of God in a way that will help those who use The Upper Room every day.

Here are some guidelines to help you make best use of The Upper Room:

1. Read the passage of Scripture. It is a good idea to read it more than once, in order to have a fuller understanding of what it is about and what you can learn from it.
2. Read the meditation. How does it relate to your own experience? Can you identify with what the writer has outlined from their own experience or understanding?
3. Pray the written prayer. Think about how you can use it to relate to people you know, or situations that need your prayers today.
4. Think about the contributor who has written the meditation. Some Upper Room users include this person in their prayers for the day.
5. Meditate on the 'Thought for the Day', the 'Link2Life' and the 'Prayer Focus', perhaps using them again as the focus for prayer or direction for action.

Why is it important to have a daily quiet time? Many people will agree that it is the best way of keeping in touch every day with the God who sustains us, and who sends us out to do his will and show his love to the people we encounter each day. Meeting with God in this way reassures us of his presence with us, helps us to discern his will for us and makes us part of his worldwide family of Christian people through our prayers.

I hope that you will be encouraged as you use the magazine regularly as part of your daily devotions, and that God will richly bless you as you read his word and seek to learn more about him.

Susan Hibbins
UK Editor

In Times of/For Help with . . .

Below is a list of entries in this copy of *The Upper Room* relating to situations or emotions with which we may need help:

Anger: May 27; June 2; July 29; Aug 16

Anxiety: May 5, 16; July 16, 27, 30

Assurance: May 5, 20; July 4, 16; Aug 19

Bible reading: May 13, 29; July 10, 15, 29; Aug 2, 27

Celebration: May 6

Change: May 1, 10, 29

Christian community: May 19, 22; June 7, 20; July 16, 29; Aug 11, 27

Compassion: June 7, 10, 16, 17

Creation/nature's beauty: May 3; June 4

Death/grief: May 24; June 7; July 13

Discouragement: July 4, 24; Aug 25

Doubt: May 13, 17, 22

Encouragement: May 10, 30; June 3, 11, 28; Aug 5, 23

Evangelism: May 19; June 2, 25; July 7; Aug 21

Failure: Aug 12

Family: May 12, 28; June 16, 24; July 5, 14; Aug 10, 11

Fear: May 30; June 12; July 4, 5, 7

Financial concerns: May 9; Aug 20

Forgiveness: May 14; July 21, 26; Aug 6

Freedom: May 5

Friendship: Aug 7, 26

Generosity: June 17; July 12, 31; Aug 20

God's goodness/love: May 2, 9, 31; June 16, 27; July 1, 6, 28; Aug 7, 29

God's presence: May 7, 18; June 4, 23; July 7, 14, 25; Aug 1, 24, 30

God's provision: May 9; July 5, 24, 30; Aug 19

Gratitude: July 11

Growth: May 25, 26; July 16, 19; Aug 25

Guidance: May 1, 27, 29; June 11; Aug 2

Healing/Illness: May 8, 21; June 13, 24, 29; Aug 29

Hope: June 26; July 13, 20; Aug 4, 5, 18

Job issues: May 2; Aug. 23

Judging: May 14; June 8

Living our faith: May 4, 15, 23; June 7, 17, 30; July 10, 27; Aug 7, 22, 31

Loss: May 24; June 7; July 13, 14, 20; Aug 12, 18

Materialism: May 9; Aug 20

Mental illness: May 28; July 25

Mission/outreach: May 15; June 5; July 18; Aug 28

New beginnings: May 1, 19, 26; June 5, 11; July 26; Aug 12

Patience: July 24, 28, 29; Aug. 5

Parenting: June 29

Peace/unrest: May 16; June 5, 6

Prayer: May 2; June 26; July 3, 15, 27; Aug 2, 10, 30

Renewal: June 13, 14; Aug 4, 12

Repentance: May 21; July 21

Salvation: June 1, 8, 18; July 8

Security: June 9, 12

Serving: May 4, 15; June 1, 7; July 2, 18, 27; Aug 14, 28

Speaking about faith: May 22; June 8; July 26; Aug 21

Social issues: May 7; June 5; July 26

Spiritual gifts: June 19, 20; Aug 21

Spiritual practices: May 8, 25, 26; July 3, 12; Aug 10, 15, 27

Stewardship: Aug 20, 22, 31

Strength: July 24

Stress: June 15

Tolerance: June 5

Tragedy: May 24; June 7, 24; July 4; Aug 15

Trust: May 11, 16, 27; June 6, 14, 28; July 5, 11, 30; Aug 1, 18

God said, 'Take off your sandals for the place where you are standing is holy ground' (Exodus 3:5).

Each year, thousands of people come to visit the historic Upper Room Chapel at our Nashville, Tennessee headquarters. Most of the time, those of us who work for *The Upper Room* are in our adjoining offices, unaware of the visitors' comings and goings. But last year Kathryn Kimball, our chapel curator, asked me to come and pray with a family.

For some time the family of a Bristol, Tennessee, woman had been coming to the chapel to pray while she saw her doctors at a nearby hospital. Sharon Wise had ALS, a vicious disease that causes total paralysis and, eventually, death. The chapel became a haven for her family during their regular medical trips. Finally, Sharon received a computer-controlled wheelchair that allowed her more mobility, and she wanted to see the chapel. When I went to meet Sharon, I was stunned to learn she was not yet 50. She seemed decades older, frail and barely able to speak a word. In the chapel, we formed a circle for prayer. As we surrounded the massive wheelchair that held this small and fragile woman, we each placed a hand on her and we began to pray. In that touch and fervent prayer, we were all lifted to a sacred place by God's love and power. It was clear to me, at that moment, that while the chapel is beautiful, it is the prayers of the faithful that invoke God's presence and reveal holy ground.

Recently, Sharon's family telephoned to tell us of her death. Her sister Debbie said the chapel meant so much to her family, and they would always remember her visit and our prayers. I'm humbled that this precious family not only found respite here, but also found a community of prayer that transcended the pages of *The Upper Room*.

Sarah Wilke
Publisher

The Editor writes...

Have you ever kept a journal? By 'journal' I don't mean a diary, or a record of your world travels, but instead a spiritual journal in which you write your reactions to, and understanding of, scripture.

Reading the Bible regularly is an intrinsic part of our spiritual life. (It is my hope that when you read the daily meditations in *The Upper Room*, you first read the passage of scripture given at the top of the page.) Our reading helps us to get to know God, to learn more about his presence in the world, to find out his will for our lives. The Bible helps us to know what Jesus' teaching is, how we are to follow his way and do the things he asks of us.

Keeping a journal goes one step further in focusing our thoughts and helping us to concentrate on what the Bible is saying to us. I have a process that I follow myself, and I would like to offer it to you, as a suggestion which you can adapt to your own circumstances.

First, I read the passage aloud. I find that if I do this, slowly, the words have more impact. As I read, I try to picture what is happening: if it is a story about Jesus, I try to imagine myself there, listening and watching as he speaks. If the passage is a psalm, I try to imagine the person who wrote it down, who they were and how they were feeling. Reading aloud helps me to do this more effectively.

Then, I read it again, looking out for a verse or verses that seem to speak especially to me. They might include words of comfort, or of challenge, or something thought-provoking that catches my attention. These are the verses I then write about in my journal. I try to think about what is God is saying me to me, how the verses address my current situation, and what I can learn from them. You don't have to write an essay, but I find that more insights come to me the more regularly I study and write, helping me to draw closer to God.

When I glance back over earlier entries it is amazing how this practice has helped me to find clarity, answers to prayer and a greater awareness of God's presence through each day and week.

Why not give the idea a try? You might be surprised by the results.

Susan Hibbins, Editor of the UK edition

PS: The Bible readings are selected with great care, and we urge you to include the suggested reading in your devotional time.

Changing Direction

Read Luke 19:1–10

Jesus answered, 'I assure you, unless someone is born anew, it's not possible to see God's kingdom.'
John 3:3 (CEB)

During a recent flight aboard a private plane, I sat in the co-pilot's seat. Five minutes into the trip, the pilot made a sharp left turn and began descending. The air-traffic controller had informed him that another aircraft was heading in our direction. This experience reminded me that the need to change direction is also part of our earthly journey, at times to steer us away from a dead-end path to one that is life-giving.

In the Bible we see this repeatedly. Having observed and listened to Jesus, the tax collector Zacchaeus realised that he wanted to know more. He invited Jesus into his home, and that encounter changed Zacchaeus. He declared a new approach to how he dealt with people, saying, 'Half of my possessions, Lord, I will give to the poor; and if I have defrauded anyone of anything, I will pay back four times as much.' Jesus also spoke to Nicodemus (see John 3) and to the woman at the well (see John 4) about changing their direction.

This still happens today. Through family members, friends, pastors and even strangers, God continues to call us in new directions. And as we pray, listen, and obey, we can trust that God will guide us on our journey through new territory.

Prayer: *Dear God, Great Shepherd of the flock, help us to follow you faithfully even when we feel unsure of the way. Amen*

Thought for the day: Jesus calls each of us to new beginnings.

Stephane Brooks (French West Indies)

It's No Bother

Read Matthew 10:29–31

Peter began to speak: 'I now realise how true it is that God does not show favouritism but accepts from every nation the one who fears him and does what is right.'
Acts 10:34–35 (NIV)

My brother-in-law had left a job he had held for more than 20 years and was looking for another one. I told him I would pray for him, but he told me not to 'bother' God, who had bigger problems to take care of. I told him that God yearns to be 'bothered'. He wants us to pray about anything—not just the big things, but everything.

I'm thankful that 'I'm too busy' or 'That's not important enough for me to deal with' aren't among God's responses. Imagine God saying, 'Can we reschedule that for next week? And instead of an hour, I can give you only 30 minutes—things are a bit hectic, what with the wars and the economic crises.'

Do you think God is more apt to listen to the prayers of church leaders or world leaders, because of who they are or the magnitude of their problems or responsibilities? Acts 10:34 says that God 'does not show favouritism'. No matter where we stand on the metaphorical ladder of importance, God listens to all of us with the same passion and concern and love.

You and I always have a standing appointment with God. So we can always tell him what's on our mind. We can 'bother' God, who's always waiting to hear from us.

Prayer: *O God, thank you for never being too busy for us. Amen*

Thought for the day: God is never too busy for us; are we too busy for him?

Link2Life: *Resolve to set up a new discipline of prayer.*

C.J. Hines (Iowa, US)

Trees of Life

Read Psalm 104:10–17
Let the fields be jubilant, and everything in them; let all the trees of the forest sing for joy.
Psalm 96:12 (NIV)

All my life I have loved trees. As a young girl, I would climb up into them, often with a favourite book in my hand. I sat happily among the canopy of leaves—my own special hiding place. Later, their cool shade on a hot summer day offered the perfect spot for picnics with my daughters. But more than these wonderful blessings, trees have been a source of inspiration to me and a reminder of God's loving providence.

As a biologist, I understand the importance of trees for the well-being of all living things. What miracles of creation they are! Trees provide us with delicious fruits, fragrant flowers, life-saving medicines and the air that we breathe. Scientists refer to trees as the 'the lungs of the earth' because trees take in carbon dioxide and give off oxygen, giving us life. In the new heaven and new earth described in scripture, the tree of life stands near the throne of God and 'the leaves of the tree are for the healing of the nations' (Revelation 22:2).

When I read God's word and look out of my window, to me trees symbolise God's majesty, wisdom and steadfast love. I am grateful for this gift that God created just for me… and for you.

Prayer: *Loving God, help us to appreciate the beauty of nature that surrounds us and reminds us of your love and faithfulness. May we— like the trees that you have created—praise you for your abundant blessings. Amen*

Thought for the day: Our planet is a living gift from God.

Diane Chambers (New Jersey, US)

Do You Love Me?

Read John 21:2–17

Little children, let's not love with words or speech but with action and truth.
1 John 3:18 (CEB)

It is early morning, and I am walking along the shores of beautiful Lake Macquarie. I can easily imagine the scene described in today's reading and perhaps include myself in the picture. The tired and disappointed disciples have been met and fed by their risen Lord. Then, as they sat around, Jesus addressed Peter for the first time since Peter denied him. 'Peter, do you love me?' Jesus asked. In reply Peter affirmed his love. Jesus' next words became Peter's motivating commission from that time on: 'Feed my sheep.'

In reality our Lord was saying, 'If you really love me, prove it by doing what I need you to do: help others to love me and encourage them on their journey.' Jesus' statement reminds me of Eliza Doolittle in *My Fair Lady* expressing her frustration by singing, 'Don't talk of love lasting through time… Show me now!' Based on how we sometimes behave, Jesus could say the same words to us: 'Don't just tell me you love me, show me. Show me by your love in daily life and relationships.'

This happens when we live close to Christ and allow him to nourish us.

Prayer: *Gracious God, we thank you that even when our love is feeble, your love for us remains strong and unchanging. Help us to grow in our love for you and to express that love each day by serving you in serving those around us. Amen*

Thought for the day: If I truly love Christ, my actions will show it.

Bill Willis (New South Wales, Australia)

Released

Read Romans 7:21—8:4

There is now no condemnation for those who are in Christ Jesus.
Romans 8:1 (NIV)

My daughter-in-law grew up with a dog named Buddy, who was kept outside on a long lead between two trees. Daily he was released for a taste of freedom. If only Buddy had recognised that he was free! Although he was released from his lead, he continued to run back and forth between the two trees as if nothing had changed.

When I glance in the mirror, I sometimes catch a glimpse of Buddy. It's not a wet snout or scruffy hair that catches my eye but a similar refusal to enjoy the freedom that's been provided for me. Divorced twice by the age of 27 and with two little boys in tow, I was overwhelmed by feelings of shame and condemnation. I kept running back and forth between my past mistakes, as if confined by a lead that kept me from moving beyond that small area.

But when I read and truly believed Romans 8:1, I began to appreciate the freedom Christ has provided for me. I memorised the verse and spoke it aloud every time shame or condemnation tugged at my heart. I now choose to believe God's truth: no matter how we feel, we are free to move beyond our mistakes. We can run in the unlimited freedom of God's truth, confident of his love and acceptance.

Prayer: *Dear Lord, help us to choose truth over feelings, which often lead us astray. Thank you for the freedom you provide for us through Jesus Christ. Amen*

Thought for the day: Freedom comes with knowing and believing that God loves us as we were—and are.

Cathy Baker (South Carolina, US)

Are You Rejoicing Yet?

Read Philippians 4:4–7

Rejoice in the Lord always; again I will say, Rejoice.
Philippians 4:4 (NRSV)

During my summer holidays I work as a leader and trainer for an indoor challenge-and-fitness centre. Sunday school classes and birthday parties are held at the centre, where participants enjoy rope climbing, obstacle courses and other competitions. When I first meet my assigned groups and explain the rules, I try to show excitement in order to get them ready for the games. I always shout in an animated voice, 'Raise your hand if you're ready for some fun!' Usually only one or two people raise their hands. I tell them, 'Well then, fun will come to you!' The difference is that for those who raised their hands, enjoyment starts immediately; the others have to wait.

People are often bogged down with the cares of life and have difficulty rejoicing. Paul told his readers that someday they'd be redeemed and ushered into God's kingdom. But why wait until then to rejoice? He invites us to begin rejoicing now.

Prayer: *Dear God, help us to experience the joy of living in your kingdom, beginning at this moment. As Jesus taught us, we pray, 'Our Father which art in heaven, Hallowed be thy name. Thy kingdom come. Thy will be done, as in heaven, so in earth. Give us day by day our daily bread. And forgive us our sins; for we also forgive every one that is indebted to us. And lead us not into temptation; but deliver us from evil.'* Amen*

Thought for the day: Knowing God brings us joy here and now.

Derek Baird (Texas, US)

     * Luke 11:2–4 (KJV)

Straw

Read Exodus 5:6–9
Let them curse, but you will bless. Let my assailants be put to shame; may your servant be glad.
Psalm 109:28 (NRSV)

Several years ago, people from the former Soviet republics had to register in Russia or apply for citizenship. The department accepted applications two days a week for three hours. To be received at the 9:00a.m. session, people started standing in a queue at 5:00a.m., and even then sometimes they did not make it to the front of the queue.

On the day I was registering, I discovered that to avoid arguments those who were on their second day of waiting had compiled a list to show who was next. However, periodically, the head of the department came out and destroyed the list in an angry frenzy. Then the queue was thrown into disarray.

This situation reminded me of the passage above when Pharaoh laid heavier work on the Hebrew people by requiring them to go out and gather their own straw. I sensed the same disdain in the actions of the department head. Anger and indignation flooded up in me. But I kept repeating to myself that God would take care of me. Pharaoh oppressed the people of Israel, but God made them a chosen people. Often people who have power can make our lives difficult. But how wonderful that God is with us!

Prayer: *Dear God, give us humility and patience to withstand the difficulties and sufferings that others inflict on us. Amen*

Thought for the day: We don't have to stand in a queue to enter the kingdom of God.

Fedor Kim (Pskov, Russia)

PRAYER FOCUS: THOSE LIVING UNDER OPPRESSIVE REGIMES

Spiritual Rehabilitation

Read 2 Peter 1:3–11

His divine power has given us everything needed for life and godliness, through the knowledge of him who called us by his own glory and goodness.

2 Peter 1:3 (NRSV)

A number of years ago, I had a heart attack. My doctors performed a bypass operation and then prescribed medication and an exercise routine. After a few weeks the doctors told me to continue with the exercise regularly, and that with proper care I could expect to have good health.

As I thought about what the doctors had prescribed for me— medication and exercise—I realised that I need regular 'exercise' to maintain my spiritual health as well.

Often, we can lose enthusiasm for our faith and fall back to our old, lethargic ways. The apostle Peter was afraid that recently converted Christians would return to their old ways and stumble in their discipleship. When such times come upon us, the Bible can be a valuable resource to hold us steady and point us back to the way of Christ. Having a daily devotional time, such as reading *The Upper Room* and studying the Bible, can keep us from stumbling and move us on toward the abundant life Jesus promised.

Prayer: *Dear Lord, we yearn for the determination to pursue what is necessary to strengthen us in our journey. Amen*

Thought for the day: God gives us the strength we need—one day at a time.

Edwin C. Wentz (Pennsylvania, US)

Beyond Comparison

Read Matthew 20:1–16

The landowner said, 'Are you envious because I am generous?'
Matthew 20:15 (NRSV)

In our reading for today, Jesus tells of a man who hired different workers at different times of the day: morning, noon and evening. When it was time for the workers to receive the wages promised to them, those who had worked all day were upset that those who came later were paid just as much as they. The employer told them he had done no wrong, that he paid each one what he had promised.

So what caused these all-day workers to be upset? They compared their situations to someone else's. If they had not compared, they would not have been dissatisfied.

Sometimes, looking at someone else's life, I become dissatisfied because theirs looks richer and fuller than mine. Maybe they have the kinds of relationships that I long for. Or maybe they have luxuries that seem unattainable to me. When we compare ourselves to someone else, we may end up feeling better than they, which can fill us with pride; or we may end up feeling worse, which can fill us with insecurity and jealousy.

The parable we read today teaches us that focusing on what others have or do not have leaves us feeling empty. If we focus instead on the goodness of God and how trustworthy and wonderful he is, we will find that the spiritual life offers riches beyond comparison.

Prayer: *Dear heavenly Father, help us to trust that you will sustain us. Amen*

Thought for the day: Looking to God makes us spiritually rich.

Kimberly Long (Texas, US)

Run a Little

Read Mark 2:1–12

The Lord said to Joshua, 'I hereby command you: Be strong and courageous; do not be frightened or dismayed, for the Lord your God is with you wherever you go.'
Joshua 1:9 (NRSV)

When our son was around six years old, he would sometimes stop as we made our way home from our shop, saying, 'Dad, I'm too tired to walk.' I would answer, 'Then you can run a little.' That was one of those typical illogical answers that a child sometimes gets from an adult. To be honest, I said it in order to distract him. But to my surprise he restored his energy by changing pace, and he was not tired any more.

We all can sometimes lose our energy simply because we get stuck at a certain pace. We form our lives in certain routines, doing business as usual. That's why I admire the paralysed man in this story from Mark's Gospel. When Jesus told him to stand up and walk, he had the courage to do so. Jesus asked him not only to change pace but to do something he certainly was not used to doing.

Persevering in the faith requires us to be willing to listen to God's voice calling us to change our routines, to do something we have not done before, and to enter areas we could never have imagined. Such a change of pace takes courage. But 'The one who calls you is faithful', and will give us the grace we need to change (1 Thessalonians 5:24).

Prayer: *Trustworthy God, help us to be so still that we can hear your voice, and give us the courage to change pace, to move where you call us. Amen*

Thought for the day: Where is God calling me to try something new?

Hans Vaxby (Moscow, Russia)

PRAYER FOCUS: THOSE STRUGGLING WITH GOD'S CALL

All Safe

Read Luke 15:3–7

Jesus said, 'My sheep hear my voice. I know them, and they follow me.'
John 10:27 (NRSV)

I grew up on a farm where we had many different animals. By far the most labour-intensive of these were the sheep. Caring for the sheep required much more work than taking care of our cattle. The sheep had to be checked on every day. Individual sheep would wander away from the flock and get lost, and lambs would get separated from their mothers. Whenever this happened there would be loud and plaintive bleating from the sheep, which would end only when one of us went to the field and brought the wandering sheep back to the flock. I have many memories of my parents pouring out feed for the sheep and then counting them to make sure that all were safe.

Whenever I hear Jesus described as a shepherd, I smile. We humans are like those difficult, wandering sheep—the ones who need so much care and tending, the ones who get lost so easily and need to be rounded up and brought back by a caring shepherd. How patient and kind shepherds have to be! But isn't that how Christ is with us, always willing to seek us and bring us back to the fold? When we stray and get lost, Christ loves us enough to look for us and bring us home.

Prayer: *Dear Lord, we thank you that you are always willing to look for us, find us and bring us back to your fold. Amen*

Thought for the day: Stay close to the Shepherd.

Link2Life: *Investigate an initiative that helps your local farming community.*

Abigail Gary (New Jersey, US)

A Letter from Mother

Read 1 John 4:9–16

As a mother comforts her child, so I will comfort you; you shall be comforted in Jerusalem.
Isaiah 66:13 (NRSV)

My mother died a few days after my fourth birthday. The only knowledge I have of her comes from stories my family tells.

When I was a teenager, my dad handed me an envelope. Inside was a letter Mother had written to me before she passed away. I read her handwritten note: 'I want to tell you how very much I love you and how I wanted and waited for you. You probably won't remember too much about me as the years go by, but I want you to grow into a fine young man, to be always mindful of God, and to ask for God's direction. Remember your mother loved you with all her heart and will always be with you in spirit.'

To be loved by someone I don't remember is a strange, wonderful feeling. Actually, we all can know what it feels like. My mother's love is but a reflection of the love of God, our parent, who has yearned for us from the beginning of time.

The Bible is a letter from God to us, reminding us of the love that mysteriously embraces us until we see God face to face. As Jesus said, 'Remember, I am with you always, to the end of the age' (Matthew 28:20).

Prayer: *Dear Lord, thank you for love that holds us close to you, even when we are unaware of you. As you have held us with such strength, may we reach out to others in Jesus' name. Amen*

Thought for the day: God loves us beyond anything we can imagine.

Gregory M. Weeks (Missouri, US)

PRAYER FOCUS: CHILDREN WHO HAVE LOST THEIR MOTHER

Life-giving Water

Read John 4:7–15

It is the God who said, 'Let light shine out of darkness,' who has shone in our hearts to give the light of the knowledge of the glory of God in the face of Jesus Christ.
2 Corinthians 4:6 (NRSV)

During my college days I was zealous in my studies and my attempts to find work. Yet my spirit felt hungry and dry. While believing that being employed by a first-rate company would bring me happiness, I also had other questions: What is the purpose of my existence? What meaning is there in my giving myself to this work? Life is limited to one time; therefore, I wanted to devote my life to something with real value.

I knew there should be something more important for me to learn, and I have been always seeking that true teaching. Then I encountered the words of Jesus in the Bible. Jesus offered me water that satisfies my spiritual thirst and became 'a spring of water gushing up to eternal life'. Before, I had seen God as distant from me. Now, I have a very close relationship, like a father and daughter.

Now that nagging uneasiness is gone. My heart is content. I worship 'in spirit and truth' (John 4:23), and I am enveloped in God's love. I give heartfelt thanks to God who shines in my heart and displaces the darkness of the world with the light of Christ.

Prayer: *O God, thank you for salvation. Deliver us from spiritual hunger and thirst as we worship you in spirit and truth. Amen*

Thought for the day: Only God can satisfy our spiritual thirst and give us eternal life.

Sachie Yoshimoto (Tokyo, Japan)

Two Lost Sons

Read Luke 15:11–32

Do not judge, and you will not be judged. Do not condemn, and you will not be condemned. Forgive, and you will be forgiven.
Luke 6:37 (NIV)

I've always loved the parable of the lost son because it is a great illustration of God's limitless grace, mercy and forgiveness. However, while many see this as a parable about the younger son, the story begins, 'There was a man who had two sons.' When I first read this story, I felt sympathy for the older son, who obeyed his father, worked hard and did the right things. We can understand why he was upset about the party his father gave in honour of his selfish, immature younger brother.

I have come to see in the older brother sins of the heart—jealousy, self-righteousness, resentment and judgment. These might not be as obvious as the outward sins of the younger brother, but they can be just as dangerous, especially since we tend to overlook them in ourselves.

The parable is a great message of love, forgiveness and grace toward the younger son. But actually its message about the older son is just as important. Jesus said earlier in the book of Luke: 'Do not judge, and you will not be judged. Do not condemn, and you will not be condemned. Forgive, and you will be forgiven' (6:37). These are great words to live by.

Prayer: *Dear God, help us to forgive as you do. Amen*

Thought for the day: To whom do I need to offer grace?

Link2Life: *Telephone your brother or sister today.*

John D. Bown (Minnesota, US)

Inconvenient Discipleship

Read Mark 8:34–38
The king will answer them, 'Truly I tell you, just as you did it to one of the least of these who are members of my family, you did it to me.'
Matthew 25:40 (NRSV)

The Christian ministry where I work serves those in need by giving food and clothing and meeting other basic needs. One Saturday as my husband and I were on our way to a business associate's company picnic, my mobile phone rang. One of my clients told me, weeping, that she had absolutely nothing to feed her children.

My first thought was, 'This is my day off, and I want to enjoy it with my husband.' But then the Lord reminded me I am a Christian all the time, not just when it is convenient. I jotted down the woman's address, and we headed to the food bank. We also stopped at our house to get some meat for the family.

When we arrived at the client's home, two of her children ran out to greet us with loving hugs. As we brought sacks of groceries into the kitchen, the young mother stood crying and gave both of us a thank you hug as well.

Sometimes I am tempted not to respond to a call from God that is inconvenient or unpleasant. But then the Lord reminds me to take up my cross and follow Jesus—24/7.

Prayer: *Dear Lord, help us to follow you whenever and wherever you call us. Fill us with overflowing love for those in need. Amen*

Thought for the day: Do I follow Jesus only when it is convenient?

Link2Life: *Become a volunteer at a local soup kitchen, or make regular contributions to that ministry.*

Lissa Stressman Smith (Michigan, US)

Calm Shining

Read Isaiah 43:1–4

When you pass through the waters, I will be with you; and through the rivers, they shall not overwhelm you; when you walk through fire you shall not be burned, and the flame shall not consume you.
Isaiah 43:2 (NRSV)

I was driving to one of our firm's subsidiaries. It is quite a distance away, but traffic was light. While crossing a bridge, I noticed a significant difference between the landscape behind me and the one I was approaching. The vegetation ahead was richer than that behind me and featured a riot of colours in hues of green and yellow.

Until this point in the trip, I had been churning inside as I thought about my work performance. My company expected better results; and as much as I tried, my efforts did not match their expectations. Now, as I crossed the bridge, I remembered that God always accompanies us as we travel through troubled waters. As I reflected more on this, my spirit lifted quickly. I felt invigorated, as if I had taken in a breath of fresh air. I thanked God for standing by me during the difficult times and guiding me to a place of peace.

Prayer: *Merciful God, help us to remember that you always guide us through the storms of life and on to safety. Amen*

Thought for the day: God guides us through troubled waters to peace.

Luis Alberto Jones (Chubut, Argentina)

Measuring Up

Read Jeremiah 9:23–24

The world and its cravings are passing away, but the person who does the will of God remains forever.
1 John 2:17 (CEB)

The Lord has blessed me, enabling me to be a wife, a mum and a grandmother. However, I have struggled from time to time with low self-esteem. Because I do not have a college education or a career outside my home, sometimes I see myself as not having anything to offer the world. Other people have so much more to offer, it seems.

Recently, as I read Jeremiah 9:23–24, I experienced an epiphany; I grasped a new perspective on how we should evaluate ourselves. God said we are not to boast in the wisdom we possess, the strength we have or the riches we've accumulated. Our education and whatever career or job we have are included as part of our wisdom and possessions. Just as we are not to boast, we are also not to be ashamed of our lack of a college education or a high-status job or career. If our value to the body of Christ could be measured, it should be measured according to our service to others.

Prayer: *Dear Lord Jesus, you came and served the world. Help us to see the ways we can follow your example in serving others. Amen*

Thought for the day: Each one of us is valuable to the body of Christ.

Karenn Voorhees (Kansas, US)

God's Touch

Read 2 Corinthians 1:3–4

I can do all things through him who strengthens me.
Philippians 4:13 (NRSV)

We have a new puppy, a Labrador retriever named Holly. We spend a lot of time swinging in the hammock while Holly explores the back garden in the comfort of our presence. If playing on the decking, she often will move close to our legs and eventually sit on someone's foot as she chews her bone. If we move while she is out on the lawn playing, she stops immediately and checks to see where we are. Our presence gives her the confidence to explore.

Holly's behaviour reminds me of my relationship with God. I explore life—sometimes without any thought of his presence. But often, especially when life throws a challenge my way, I need the comfort of God's touch; I need to know that he is close by and that I matter. I need to know that God is working diligently for good in all situations in my life.

God's touch may come through a hug from another person, through something that I read in the Bible or through a timely devotion in *The Upper Room*. Sometimes I sense God's touch in the still, small voice that occasionally comes when I least expect it—but I sense its message with startling clarity. In whatever form it comes, that touch gives my life warmth and colour and fills me with confidence that through God's power at work in me I can do all that he asks of me.

Prayer: *Dear Lord, help us to look for the many ways you touch us with your love and care every day. Amen*

Thought for the day: How do I experience God's touch?

Cathy Fooshee (Kansas, US)

A Different Ending

Read Acts 2:1–22, 41–42
When the day of Pentecost had come, they were all together in one place.
Acts 2:1 (NRSV)

Hours after the last supper, the disciples were put to the test—and they failed. They abandoned Jesus when the soldiers came, denied they knew him and mostly hid while he died on the cross. They were so cowardly that they did what we probably would have done, perhaps what anyone with common sense would have done.

The story must have seemed familiar to people living in Israel during Roman times. Others had claimed to be the messiah and were executed by the authorities as their followers scattered. But this time the story had a different ending. This time, those who had fled came back to proclaim more loudly than ever that the executed man was really the Saviour. Something had profoundly changed the followers since the night they forsook their leader. What was it? They had seen the risen Lord.

These failed followers had bickered among themselves over places of honour, had misunderstood Jesus and had tried to tempt him to the easy way. But then the Holy Spirit descended upon these former cowards in flames. And these all-too-human followers boldly spoke in dozens of tongues to tell the good news. The disciples had become the Church. We call it Pentecost.

Prayer: *Dear gracious God, thank you for the message of Easter. Make us bold witnesses of your grace. Amen*

Thought for the day: The power of God can transform cowards into bold witnesses.

Drew Sappington (Florida, US)

No Performance Necessary

Read John 1:14–17

From [the Word's] fullness we have all received grace upon grace.
John 1:16 (CEB)

My granddaughters were to take part in a classical ballet competition. However, before the ballet, we were told that a troupe of five-year-old girls would perform individually. Four girls came on stage, one after the other. Then came the turn of Number 5. The music for the dance was 'Me and My Teddy Bear'. But no little girl appeared. Instead we heard her crying.

Later in the programme all the dancers lined up on stage. To our delight, each little girl was given a medal on a ribbon, including Number 5, who, pale and tear-stained, was clutching her teddy bear. We saw no tears now but instead a watery smile.

That's like grace, I thought. We don't have to perform; we don't have to earn God's approval. Grace is the unmerited love of God. It's sheer gift, a free expression of God's love for us.

Prayer: *Dear Lord, we thank you for the riches of your grace. Grant that we may receive these riches graciously and live our gratitude by offering gracious acceptance to those we meet. We pray as Jesus taught us, saying, 'Our Father which art in heaven, Hallowed be thy name. Thy kingdom come. Thy will be done in earth, as it is in heaven. Give us this day our daily bread. And forgive us our debts, as we forgive our debtors. And lead us not into temptation, but deliver us from evil: For thine is the kingdom, and the power, and the glory, for ever. Amen.'**

Thought for the day: To receive graciously brings blessings both to those who give and to those who receive.

Dorothy O'Neill (South Australia, Australia)

PRAYER FOCUS: CHILDREN IN COMPETITIONS
* Matthew 6:9–13 (KJV)

Open for Healing

Read Psalm 51:1–7

If we confess our sins, he who is faithful and just will forgive us our sins and cleanse us from all unrighteousness.
1 John 1:9 (NRSV)

Friends told me that my sudden illness was an allergic reaction, but I didn't really believe them because I'd never had allergies. Finally, with a high fever and barely able to move, I begged my wife to take me to the hospital. I remember saying, 'I suppose they are right. I must have some sort of allergy.'

The hospital staff isolated the problem and took corrective measures that relieved my physical distress. Later it struck me that until I admitted my problem, little could be done to save me from it. I had to be open to the remedy for my condition.

Something similar is true for us as sinners. Until we admit that we have sinned, we can never open our hearts to accept God's forgiving grace that is the remedy for sin. I once heard a minister say, 'The hardest step in the act of redemption is the step where the sinner accepts the need for it.' Only when we admit that we are sinners can we accept God's grace offered as a remedy for our sinfulness.

Prayer: *Dear Father, we have sinned, and we fear that you will reject us because of it. Help us to accept your grace and draw close to you. Amen*

Thought for the day: The moment we turn from our sin, we will find God's grace.

Gale Richards (Iowa, US)

Understanding

Read John 20:24–29

The boy's father exclaimed, 'I do believe; help me overcome my unbelief!'
Mark 9:24 (NIV)

Recently I was with some friends discussing our understanding of God. One person always referred to him using the phrase, 'the God I don't understand'. Another said she was truly glad there was mystery involved in understanding God. The third person said he had been searching everywhere for God and in every way possible, but he could not find him. Therefore, he decided to stop searching and let God find him. Then he added, 'It worked!'

Listening to these comments made me think of Thomas' experience of questioning and seeking. And then I remembered the father who had asked for his son to be healed and how he answered Jesus by saying, 'I do believe; help my unbelief!'

At times I am like each one in my group of friends, and sometimes I am like the people I read about in scripture. I find comfort in knowing that people in the Bible grappled with the same feelings and challenges we experience today. God always knows where we are. When we are still (see Psalm 46:10) and make ourselves available to God, we are saying 'Here I am, God. Find me!' At times, I see his presence revealed through other people or even through nature (such as when a butterfly lights on my hand and stays there). I am grateful for the mystery of the God I don't fully understand. And I'm equally grateful that when I cannot find God, I know that he can and will find me.

Prayer: *Thank you, God, that you never change. My understanding of you may change, but you forever remain the same. Amen*

Thought for the day: Perceptions may change, but God remains constant.

Patricia A. Simmons (Missouri, US)

Tomorrow's Pharisee

Read Luke 11:37–44

Jesus said, 'Woe to you Pharisees, because you give God a tenth of your mint, rue and all other kinds of garden herbs, but you neglect justice and the love of God.'
Luke 11:42 (NIV)

A pastor of mine once said, 'The Christians of one generation tend to become the Pharisees of the next.' The Pharisees had started out on the right path; they wanted to live for God. But keeping the law became an end in itself. They forgot that the law was meant to draw them closer to God.

Today's reading shows what happens when our focus on outward cleanliness becomes an obsession, blocking out the more important part of the inner life. Jesus' words cause us to step back and look carefully at what we're doing and why we're doing it. The three 'woes' in today's reading remind us not to focus on appearances while the inner life is in disrepair.

The first tells us that if we love God, we will desire justice and give to the poor. Then Jesus says that if we are humble, we will not care about having the 'important' seats. Finally, if we neglect the inner life, Jesus tells us, we will become like an unmarked grave, trampled underfoot. But if we nurture it, we will be vital and spiritually alive.

Prayer: *Dear God, help us to remain focused on loving and serving you. Amen*

Thought for the day: How can I focus less on keeping the rules and more on loving God?

Dan G. Johnson (Florida, US)

From Death to Resurrection

Read John 20:1–10

Cast your cares on the Lord and he will sustain you.
Psalm 55:22 (NIV)

On Good Friday, John stood at the cross beside Mary, the mother of Jesus. Together they faced what was surely the worst day of their lives, as the man they loved suffered and died. We next read of John's racing to the empty tomb on Sunday. But where had he been on Saturday? Did he try to comfort Mary and to deal with his own brokenness? Did he spend time with the other disciples as they struggled to make sense of recent events? Did he go for a long walk, reliving the past days? If only we could have reassured him, 'Hang on, John, resurrection is coming. Things will get better.' But he probably wouldn't have believed us.

One of the worst days of my life came when I received my cancer diagnosis. People told me, 'It will get better'; but I didn't believe them. Years later, I have a ministry to hurting people, and I'm a published author. Yes, my life got better. But I didn't believe it would when people told me.

Loss and death come to all of us. When we are broken and confused, the future seems messy. When that's our situation, we can hang on in assurance that resurrection is coming. God says so.

Prayer: *Dear Lord, when we face tough days, help us to remember that you've promised to bring good out of all our circumstances. Amen*

Thought for the day: Even when we see only death, God promises resurrection.

Shirley M. Corder (Eastern Cape, South Africa)

In Training

Read Hebrews 12:1–13
Very early in the morning, while it was still dark, Jesus got up, left the house and went off to a solitary place, where he prayed.
Mark 1:35 (NIV)

In my area, the month of June kicks off the season of triathlon racing. These contests of varying distances include swimming, cycling and running and are held one after the other. Over the last five years I have competed in triathlons and will participate again this year.

In order to complete a triathlon, an athlete needs to prepare for it. Workouts that balance all three areas are better for the body and more helpful in completing the races than are workouts that focus on just one area.

A spiritual journey is a lot like a triathlon. To engage fully in the spiritual journey we need balance in prayer, Bible study and worship. These three activities will strengthen our spiritual lives so that we can accomplish what the writer of Hebrews calls 'the race marked out for us' (12:1). Some might add a fourth area—service. But I am a firm believer that service is actually an outward expression of prayer, Bible study and worship.

When we train by praying, reading the Bible and worshipping with others, we can persevere in the race marked out for us, the race that leads to an experience of God that is eternal.

Prayer: *Dear Source of all love, fill us with desire, strength and perseverance to grow in Christ-likeness. Amen*

Thought for the day: How do I 'work out' spiritually?

Link2Life: *Start today to keep a journal that records what you learn from your Bible reading.*

Charles D. Kelsey (Iowa, US)

Filled with God's Spirit

Read John 3:1–8

Jesus said, 'The wind blows where it chooses, and you hear the sound of it, but you do not know where it comes from or where it goes. So it is with everyone who is born of the Spirit.'
John 3:8 (NRSV)

As the outdoor, Easter sunrise service began, I noticed a hot-air balloon lying limp on the ground. When the minister started the sermon, someone began to pump hot air into the balloon, and soon it expanded into brilliant colour, ready to rise, symbolising the risen Christ.

Watching the balloon, I reflected on my past and realised that my life had once been like that empty balloon. When our children were grown, I stopped attending church. As time passed, I sensed something was missing in my day-to-day existence. I felt unfulfilled. When I made the decision to worship again, my life began to change. The spirit of God flooded into my being.

My spiritual journey took me to Bible studies and on mission trips. Participating in small study groups gave me the opportunity to grow and learn from other church members. My days took on new meaning and purpose. Like that once-empty balloon, my once-empty life is now filled—with the grace, love and strength of God.

Prayer: *Dear God, fill the voids in us with your presence. Amen*

Thought for the day: The presence of Christ makes us feel alive.

Bob Beaudoin (Connecticut, US)

PRAYER FOCUS: THOSE WHO DO NOT ATTEND CHURCH

Potholes

Read Psalm 27

In the Lord I take refuge.
Psalm 11:1 (NIV)

I winced, gritted my teeth and muttered under my breath. The car rattled and rocked. I had hit yet another pothole on my way to work. The holes varied in depth as well as width. Some were avoidable; some were not. Signs warned drivers about some of them; new ones caught me by surprise time and time again.

Angry after another jolting journey home, I reached for pen and paper, ready to vent my fury via a letter to the local newspaper. With pen poised, I paused. Although the potholes are a problem that needs to be addressed, God revealed to me the true cause of my anger: my son was experiencing a difficult time, and I felt helpless. I could do nothing but sit back, watch and pray. I returned the pen and paper to the drawer, my agitation having subsided.

Knowing Christ doesn't guarantee a completely smooth ride, but with him we can endure life's uneven road. He endured a much harder road to the cross. Because of that great love, he will guide us through our journey and provide us with what we need to reach our destination.

Prayer: *Dear Lord, give us courage and strength to endure hardship, in the knowledge that you walk beside us, step by step. Amen*

Thought for the day: Christ loves our loved ones even more than we do.

Julia Cutting (East Yorkshire, England)

My Father's Love

Read Ephesians 6:1–4

Honour your father and your mother, so that your days may be long in the land that the Lord your God is giving you.
Exodus 20:12 (NRSV)

When I was 16, I was told for the first time that my grandfather had spent a year in a mental hospital before I was born. Grandpa had always seemed a bit odd to me, but I never thought he was mentally ill.

When I asked my dad why he had not told me this earlier, his response revealed something important about love. He acknowledged that his father was mentally ill and that the disease had caused much pain. But he had not told me about the illness. He did not want me to judge or be frightened of my grandfather. He wanted me to love his dad as my grandfather, as he had loved him as his dad.

The fourth commandment tells us to honour our father and mother and follows with the promise: 'that it may be well with you and you may live long on the earth'. Twenty-five years have passed since I learned about my grandfather, and I have kept that moment alive as a testament to what loving and honouring a parent means. I saw in my dad a testament to the love of God, who loves us no matter what our circumstances, illnesses or past acts.

Prayer: *Dear God, thank you for those who have loved us. Direct us to show others how to love sacrificially and unconditionally. Amen*

Thought for the day: Love looks beyond human frailty to see the image of God in each person.

Matthew L. Reger (Ohio, US)

A Fixed Point

Read Deuteronomy 11:16–21
The Lord says, 'Fix these words of mine in your hearts and minds.'
Deuteronomy 11:18 (NIV)

Recently I went for a nostalgic drive through my old neighbourhood and was shocked to find that I hardly recognised it. The landmarks I remembered were no longer there, and soon I was hopelessly lost.

Life in the 21st century is a bit like that. Many landmarks that guided us are no longer here. We find ourselves feeling ill at ease in a world where boundaries are few and ideas about morality have changed, leaving us often in confusion.

In earlier times, navigators at sea plotted their course according to certain, fixed points—a star, a headland or some other permanent feature. As Christians, we also have such reference points. Our God is unchanging throughout the millennia, and the Bible provides eternal truth that will outlast all fads and philosophies. God's truths provide the only reference we need to guide us through life. And we are entrusted with the holy task of teaching these truths to others.

Prayer: *Dear Father, enable us to base our lives on your timeless truths, not on the passing fads of any culture. Amen*

Thought for the day: 'Jesus Christ is the same yesterday and today and forever' (Hebrews 13:8).

Colette Williams (South Australia, Australia)

Cricket Catching

Read Luke 5:17–26
The Spirit God gave us does not make us timid, but gives us power, love and self-discipline.
2 Timothy 1:7 (NIV)

As a boy, I mastered the art of catching fish bait. First, I had to find a patch of tall grass. Then I walked systematically through the grass, with one foot sweeping forward in a slow scythe-like motion. Scared crickets would leap, at which point I would crouch, cup one hand and pounce.

Somewhere along the line, I lost my passion for catching crickets —and, on a much larger scale, for mastering new things. From fear of failure or disapproval, I now stay safely in my comfort zone. In fact, as an adult, I live more like a cricket than a person, hiding and leaping in fear.

Throughout the Gospels, Jesus says, 'Fear not.' He appreciates faith-driven courage and boldness, such as that of the paralytic's friends (Luke 5:17–26). In 2 Timothy, Paul reminds Timothy to rekindle the gift of God that was in him. Although Timothy was loyal and dependable, he apparently struggled with being timid, just as I do. Paul urged him to remember that God's power was at work in him. In times when I feel small and scared, like a cricket, it's comforting to know that God's powerful spirit is also in me, encouraging me, 'Take heart! I have overcome the world' (John 16:33).

Prayer: *Dear God, please help us to follow your will boldly, no matter how scary and uncomfortable it may seem. Amen*

Thought for the day: Since God has given me a spirit of power, I can be bold today.

Stephen Bishop (North Carolina, US)

PRAYER FOCUS: THOSE LIMITED DAILY BY THEIR FEARS

No Insignificance

Read Psalm 139:1–18

Are not two sparrows sold for a penny? Yet not one of them will fall to the ground apart from your Father. And even the hairs of your head are all counted.
Matthew 10:29–30 (NRSV)

No one on earth is insignificant. God created each of us unique. We have distinct fingerprints, voices, eyes and DNA. No one has ever been exactly like you; nor will anyone in the future ever be exactly like you. Although your descendants will carry parts of your DNA, none will be like you.

Our Creator provides salvation and offers a relationship with us personally. God even knows the number of hairs on our head. Your name and mine are engraved on the palm of his hand (see Isaiah 49:16). Even if a mother could forget her child, God will never forget us (see Isaiah 49:15). He makes a covenant with each of us—a binding agreement; God loves us even before we decide to love him.

God's Son, Jesus, died on the cross for you and for me. We are important to God. Throughout the Bible we read that he cares about individuals—the one lost sheep (Luke 15), the Samaritan woman despised by her own people (John 4), the widow whose only son had died (Luke 7), and many more. God doesn't ask us to be great by human standards. All we are asked to do is to love him in the ways that we can.

Prayer: *Loving Lord, help us to see ourselves the way you see us. In Jesus' name we pray. Amen*

Thought for the day: Each of us is called to love God uniquely.

Isabella Meyer (Western Cape, South Africa)

Be Blessed

Read Ephesians 1:3–10
There will be showers of blessing.
Ezekiel 34:26 (NIV)

It's 5:30 a.m. on a Saturday, and I'm awake. *Really, God?*

A group from the church would be leaving at 6 to go to cook and serve breakfast to the homeless. On Thursday I had told the preacher that I had plans for Saturday. Never mind that my planned activity did not begin until 10 and that we would have finished serving by then. Haven't I already helped several times this year? Other people need to take a turn.

All these thoughts and more ran through my head. I tried to make up excuses. But since I was wide awake, I felt that God wanted me to go. I never woke up this early on a Saturday normally. Despite feeling guilty for resisting God's nudge, I was still lying in bed. Then I realised that whether I went or not, God would not love me any more or any less. My salvation would not be any less secure. This assurance got me out of bed with joy in my heart and a desire to serve.

Cooking and serving breakfast to hungry people and working alongside my brothers and sisters was a blessing. God didn't wake me to do a task; he woke me to give me a blessing.

Prayer: *Dear Giver of all good things, thank you for the blessings that you shower on us. And thank you for loving us no matter what we do. Amen*

Thought for the day: When God sends us to serve, he also sends us a blessing.

Link2Life: *Find out this week if there is a ministry to the hungry in your area.*

Cathy Hooper (Texas, US)

Let Your Light Shine

Read Matthew 5:13–16

The Lord says, 'I will give you as a light to the nations, that my salvation may reach to the end of the earth.'
Isaiah 49:6 (NRSV)

I was travelling to church by bus one Sunday morning wearing my best church clothes and holding my Bible. The conductor bumped into me twice as he was giving change to a customer. I wanted to shout at him in the strongest terms, but something restrained my tongue. I noticed his eyes were bloodshot, and I could smell alcohol on his breath.

For the moment I kept quiet, and I am glad I did. The conductor looked at me and said, 'Are you going to church? Please pray for me that I can change. I want to change.' I asked him his name, and I talked with him about the love of God. Then I prayed for him when I got off the bus.

Would I have had a chance to talk with him about God if I had scolded him or argued? I doubt it. How we choose to respond in daily situations can be a light to those around us. I thought about Jesus' words in Matthew 5:16, 'Let your light shine before others, so that they may see your good works and give glory to your Father in heaven.'

What we do or say can lead people toward God or away from him. May we choose to serve as God's lights wherever we see darkness around us.

Prayer: *Loving God, teach us to share your love and light to those around us whom we find difficult. Remind us that they too are your children and worthy of your grace. Amen*

Thought for the day: Kindness can open doors to talk about God.

Foluke Bosede Ola (Oyo, Nigeria)

Good Job!

Read Hebrews 10:23–25

A voice came from heaven, saying, 'This is my beloved Son, in whom I am well pleased.'
Matthew 3:17 (KJV)

Once a week, my two-year-old granddaughter and I go on an adventure. Before we drive to the park or to the shops, I buckle my granddaughter into her car seat. Last week, as usual, I found the task challenging. Lifting her into her car seat was awkward. I struggled to position, adjust and buckle the shoulder straps and then the safety belt. The task completed, I looked at my granddaughter—now safe and secure—and let out a deep sigh of relief. She looked up at me with big blue eyes, smiled and said, 'Good job!'

I was startled that a two-year-old knew those words, more surprised that she knew when to say them. I felt that my efforts were appreciated and realised that her parents must have been saying, 'Good job!' to her as she mastered new skills. I was pleased that she is learning to be an encourager.

God is the ultimate encourager. We hear encouragement in his words after Jesus' baptism, 'This is my beloved Son, in whom I am well pleased.' We follow God's example when we appreciate the efforts of others. Encouragers lift the spirits of struggling people. As the word implies, encouragers fill us with courage for the next challenge. We can speak encouragement to people who need to hear that their efforts are appreciated—and that is all of us.

Prayer: *Dear God, help us to encourage one another in facing the challenges of daily life. Amen*

Thought for the day: God encourages us to encourage others.

Jan Winston (Kansas, US)

Music! Music!

Read Job 38:1–7

I praise you because I am fearfully and wonderfully made.
Psalm 139:14 (NIV)

Many years ago, I had the privilege of singing in an excellent church choir. One year, the director of a college came to give us voice lessons. I learned that when middle C is struck on the piano, the bones of the inner ear vibrate exactly 256 times per second.

Our ears open to receive the music in and around us. We think as many as 50,000 thoughts a day. When we walk, we use about 200 muscles. The mystery of our birth, the mystery of the love we feel, the mystery of our identity are unfathomable. Each of us is an incredible example of creation. We are 'fearfully and wonderfully made'.

Everyday life isn't everyday. The surface of what we see and hear isn't all there is. When we laugh, when we cry, when we feel something happening inside, we open ourselves to the possibilities of seeing God more deeply. The potential of the life that we have been given is breathtaking—when we pay attention.

The possibilities are endless. The music of the presence of God is everywhere. If we open our ears, we can hear it. Yes, God is near.

Prayer: *For your glory and majesty, for the beauty of the works of your hands, for your music that fills the universe, we give you praise, O Lord. In Jesus' name we pray. Amen*

Thought for the day: Listen to the music of God's presence.

James A. Brunner (Arizona, US)

Ministry of Reconciliation

Read 2 Corinthians 5:11–21

If anyone is in Christ, there is a new creation: everything old has passed away…! All this is from God, who reconciled us to himself through Christ, and has given us the ministry of reconciliation.
2 Corinthians 5:17–18 (NRSV)

For much of the 1990s, Belfast was a scary place to be. We lived with weekly bombings, shootings and other constant threats. My children essentially grew up in a war zone. People were afraid to talk. Then I joined an interdenominational group and heard Paul's message: 'Everything has become new!' These were joyful words amid the tension and suspicion around us. And with relationship with Christ comes a task: the 'ministry of reconciliation'.

As part of our mission, I quietly attended both Catholic and Protestant churches. I discovered ways of meeting people with diverse religious affiliations and political goals. This seemed a tiny ministry compared with those who were carrying out important peace negotiations and making groundbreaking public statements.

Later, church people and politicians from all Northern Irish political positions were led by the same hope for peace. A patient commitment from the British, Irish and American governments kept that hope alive. Many people inside and outside our churches worked together across deep divisions. As we look to God for our hope, peace can thrive.

Prayer: *Dear God of forgiveness, give us patience and skill to be your agents of reconciliation wherever there is division. Amen*

Thought for the day: Keep hoping, praying and working for peace.

Mary Taylor (Northern Ireland, United Kingdom)

Contentment

Read Philippians 4:10–14

He makes me lie down in green pastures; he leads me beside still waters; he restores my soul.

Psalm 23:2–3 (NRSV)

I saw the doe long before she saw me. She was nestled on a soft patch of grass, enjoying the peace of the quiet forest. I didn't want to disturb her. She seemed perfectly content where she was.

I felt the peace I saw in that scene! But the company I worked for was in danger of going out of business, and I faced the prospect of losing my job. With the unemployment rate high, getting a new job would be no easy task.

But the Bible tells us that stress does not mean we can't find contentment. The apostle Paul learned that the way to be content in every circumstance of life is to rely on God and the strength God provides (Philippians 4:12–13). God enables us to 'lie down in green pastures' and restores our souls (Psalm 23:2–3).

I don't know what the future holds, but I do know that God will be with me every step of the way. In a world that changes daily, we find peace and contentment in believing the promises of God, who never changes.

Prayer: *Dear unchanging God, thank you for being with us through all circumstances. Please be our guide and grant us peace. Amen*

Thought for the day: We find contentment in God's presence.

Wallace Brixner, Jr (New Jersey, US)

Ordinary Acts

Read 1 Kings 19:1–12

Carry each other's burdens and so you will fulfil the law of Christ.
Galatians 6:2 (CEB)

Several years ago my young son played baseball. I loved watching the games with the other mums, especially those who were members of the church where I was a pastor. In the midst of that idyllic time, a tragedy broke the hearts of everyone in our small town. A star high-school baseball player was killed in a car crash while at a tournament with his college baseball team. He was 19 years old. His older sister, Melinda, was a member of our church.

The next summer as Melinda and I were outside watching baseball again, I asked her as I had often that year, 'How are you getting through this?' She answered, 'By God's grace. I know people are praying for me. When people send me notes or cards, when they telephone to see how I'm doing, I know their love and concern for me are answers to my prayers and pleas for support.'

We all know someone who is going through a difficult time—the loss of a job, illness or the death of a loved one. In those situations, do we sometimes look too hard for God's presence? Do we expect answers to prayer always to be dramatic? God works through acts as simple as a phone call from a friend. You and I can be the answer to someone's prayer for help and comfort.

Prayer: *Loving God, show us how to reach out to people in ordinary and simple ways. Amen*

Thought for the day: Ordinary acts can be signs of the presence of God.

Dorcas Conrad (West Virginia, US)

Do Not Judge!

Read Matthew 7:1–5

Jesus... said to his disciples, 'How hard it will be for those who have wealth to enter the kingdom of God!... [the disciples] said to one another, 'Then who can be saved?' Jesus... said, 'For mortals it is impossible, but... for God all things are possible.'
Mark 10:23, 26–27 (NRSV)

Several times I have heard Christians say to others whose attitude or behaviour they considered wrong: 'You will not be saved.' Such statements bother me, particularly when addressed to someone in response to his or her ideas or questions about faith. I think no believer should judge the faithfulness or religious sensibility of others—the way they read the Bible, the way they pray, whether or not they go to church.

Scripture teaches that God, not humans, will decide who enters the kingdom. While it is up to us to witness to our faith in Christ through our behaviour, it is not ours to judge what's in another's heart. Only God can do that.

We aspire to salvation, to eternal life, but the only one who can give it to us is the Lord, because 'for mortals [salvation] is impossible'. But 'everything is possible for God'. And God offers salvation to all.

Prayer: *Almighty Lord, you alone can bring us close to you for all eternity. Help us to lead others to know you. Amen*

Thought for the day: Rather than standing in opposition to our brothers and sisters, let us stand beside them and praise the Lord together.

Giunio Censi (Varese, Italy)

A Safe Place

Read Psalm 91:1–16

You are my hiding place; you will protect me from trouble and surround me with songs of deliverance.

Psalm 32:7 (NIV)

We live next to a river, and across from our house three strong trees grow on the riverbank. In the evening I like to watch as flocks of ibis, cormorants and other birds come to the trees to rest for the night. At times I have counted more than 60 birds flying into those trees, and yet when they are settled, not one bird can be seen. The trees offer a safe place for the night.

Like those birds, we often need a safe place—some shelter during the storms that life inevitably brings. We need a place to hide when we feel weary and worn. Just as those trees are safe resting places for the birds, so is God a refuge for me and for you, always there, a 'hiding place'. In his sheltering presence we are refreshed and restored as we pray and read the Bible.

When I look at those trees, I remember that God is always there for me—offering safety, rest, comfort and refreshment. And I am grateful.

Prayer: *Dear heavenly Father, in the busyness of life, in the good times and the bad, you are always with us. We come to you for protection and rest. Thank you. Amen*

Thought for the day: God offers us refuge in a dangerous and demanding world.

Ann Stewart (South Australia, Australia)

One Ring, No Circus

Read Mark 10:46–52

Jesus asked [Bartimaeus], 'What do you want me to do for you?' The blind man said, 'Teacher, I want to see.'

Mark 10:51 (CEB)

My four-year-old twin daughters and I were at the circus. At times the arena would go dark and a single spotlight would shine on the ringmaster. He was dressed in vibrant, flowing clothes with an extra-large hat. His voice boomed as he called attention to himself and to the next act.

The image of this ringmaster made me think of another Master. But this master, Jesus, was different. He did not stand on a box and wave his arms and shout, 'Gather round and see the miraculous. First, someone confirm that this man is really blind. Now, watch and be amazed!' Instead, Jesus simply asked him, 'What do you want me to do for you?'

Jesus' miracles were usually focused on helping someone. His miracles impress me not so much because of their display of power but because they reveal his caring heart. Multiplying fish and bread is quite amazing, but what really draws me to Jesus is that he noticed when people were tired and hungry and did something about it. He did miracles because he cared.

Prayer: *Dear Jesus, help us to follow your example and care for the people around us. Amen*

Thought for the day: Jesus' miracles prove that God cares about human needs.

Robert LaForge (New Jersey, US)

TUESDAY 11 JUNE

Making Excuses

Read Exodus 4:1–17
Moses said to the Lord, 'O my Lord, I have never been eloquent, neither in the past nor even now that you have spoken to your servant; but I am slow of speech and slow of tongue.'
Exodus 4:10 (NRSV)

When Moses was called by God, Moses' first response was, 'Who am I that I should go to Pharaoh and bring the Israelites out of Egypt?' (Exodus 3:11, NIV). God then countered all of Moses' objections about his mission. God gave him power to perform miracles and promised to go with him and teach him what to say. Moses still was not willing and wanted somebody else to be given that job. God was angry but then commissioned Aaron to speak for Moses.

My situation was something like Moses'. A couple of years ago, I was hesitant to take up a new responsibility in my organisation. I had neither academic qualifications nor the experience for the new job. I felt inadequate and fearful. At the same time, I sensed that the new assignment was something God wanted me to do. Gradually my thinking changed. Instead of considering only my limitations, I started taking into account the help from God that would be available to me. After taking some time to decide, I agreed to take the new job and prayed for guidance in doing it. God was faithful and gave me not only wisdom for the task but also power to carry it out.

Prayer: *Source of strength, help us to focus not on our limitations but on your unlimited resources. Amen*

Thought for the day: With every assignment, God also gives us ability to accomplish it.

Pramila Barkataki (Uttar Pradesh, India)

PRAYER FOCUS: THOSE WHO FEEL INADEQUATE FOR A NEW TASK

Rock in a Storm

Read Psalm 57:1–3

*The Lord is… my fortress, and my deliverer, my God, my rock in whom
I take refuge, my shield, and the horn of my salvation, my stronghold.*
Psalm 18:2 (NRSV)

We were climbing a mountain in Washington's Cascade Range.
The weather was calm, we were below snow level and the summit
was within sight. Suddenly, at about 7500 feet, we encountered a
fierce wind that made movement difficult and dangerous. Clutching
our jackets and trying to protect our eyes from blowing debris, my
climbing partner (who later became my wife) and I crawled behind
a large boulder. The rock offered protection until we could resume
our climb to the summit, where the air was clear and calm.

Our lives often follow a similar course. Challenges and uncertainty may suddenly arise, frustrating our plans and disrupting our
journey. Unemployment, loneliness and illness may confront us
when we feel least able to cope. However, when difficulties and
peril surround us, we can take shelter in the rock that is the Lord,
knowing God hears our prayers and offers refuge for us both on this
earth and for eternity.

Prayer: *Dear Lord, we thank you for being our rock during the storms of
life. We pray that we may be a blessing to others in need. Amen*

Thought for the day: When fierce winds buffet us, God is our rock
and our refuge.

Robert Boertien (Oregon, US)

The Gardener

Read John 15:1–5

The Lord will guide you continually, and satisfy your needs in parched places, and make your bones strong; and you shall be like a watered garden.
Isaiah 58:11 (NRSV)

Gardening is my husband's favourite hobby. He especially loves bringing home sick or dying plants that his colleagues have thrown away. He nurtures them by giving one of them extra water, another fertiliser. He trims off diseased leaves. Over time, he carefully restores these withered brown plants to life. Sometimes they even surprise us with blooms.

I used to grumble about the ugly plants cluttering up our windowsill. Then one day as I watched my husband working with these sick and dying plants, I saw instead Christ's hands gently caring for me.

I was broken and sick when Christ took me in. Many of us are. But he provides each of us what we need to grow. He doesn't care if we are sickly. He restores us to life, abundant life. Christ sees the promise in us when no one else does, and through his tender care, we can bloom.

Prayer: *Dear Sustainer of life, thank you for seeing beyond our brokenness. Feed us your word to make us strong, and trim off branches that don't bear fruit for you. In Jesus' name we pray. Amen*

Thought for the day: I will allow Christ to tend to my spirit today.

Link2Life: *Spend some time in a garden today and reflect on God's care.*

Heidi Gaul (Oregon, US)

Returning from Exile

Read Jeremiah 29:1–14

The Lord proclaims: When Babylon's seventy years are up, I will come and fulfil my gracious promise to bring you back to this place.
Jeremiah 29:10 (CEB)

For much of my life as a believer I have heard Jeremiah 29:11 quoted: 'I know the plans I have for you,' declares the Lord, 'plans to prosper you and not to harm you, plans to give you hope and a future' (NIV). I have been comforted by the words but have not really thought about the context in which they were expressed. This was God's reassurance to people in exile.

Because of the people's unfaithfulness, they were taken to Babylon, where they would stay for decades. Then God would bring them back to the promised land.

Knowing the context makes this verse even more meaningful to me. When I sin, discipline may come in the consequences I suffer. Or I may be 'exiled' from the comfort of close relationship with God. But I know God's faithfulness, and I know that I, like the Israelites, will be brought out of my exile as I recognise my waywardness and return to God.

Prayer: *Dear Lord, thank you for your grace given as discipline and your mercy given as forgiveness. Teach us to seek righteousness and to repent when we fall short. Amen*

Thought for the day: When we turn from our sin, God faithfully restores us.

K. Jackson Peevy (Alabama, US)

Persevere!

Read Isaiah 40:29–31

Do not fear, for I am with you; do not be dismayed, for I am your God. I will strengthen you and help you; I will uphold you with my righteous right hand.
Isaiah 41:10 (NIV)

For many years, the care and supervision of my ageing parents has been my responsibility. Although they live in their own home, I deliver groceries, plan and prepare meals, organise and order medicines, and drive them to doctors' appointments. I have put my life on hold and am often not available to my husband or children. I pray daily for physical strength, wisdom in decision-making and protection for my family.

One day, feeling overwhelmed, I pleaded with God for help. Minutes later, I switched on the radio and heard a speaker who seemed to be talking directly to me. He said, 'We all have times when we want to give up. But I am here to tell you one thing: God is present in our troubles. God loves us. And God offers us strength to persevere.' In that moment, I was reassured that God had heard my cries and would see me through this phase of my life.

Often God speaks to us through people who give us hope to move forward when the stress of living seems too much. We are called to honour our parents. With God's strong hand on me and by abundant prayer, I will find the support I need to honour them with grace and love.

Prayer: *Thank you, God, for revealing yourself to us in our weakest moments. Amen*

Thought for the day: When we are ready to give up, God is not.

RoxAnn Henry (Pennsylvania, US)

God's Kindness

Read John 13:34–35

God so loved the world that he gave his one and only Son, that whoever believes in him shall not perish but have eternal life.
John 3:16 (NIV)

My Dad was 87 when he died. He loved God, and he loved people. I miss the kindness in his eyes and his voice, his gentleness and care. He made me feel valued and important.

It wasn't always this way. When I was 30, he apologised to me for showing more attention to my brothers than to me when we were children. I had felt rejected and unimportant. Since then, God used my dad in wonderful ways to show me love. Through my dad, I came to understand the kindness of Jesus. He became more attentive to me; he listened well, showing an active interest in my life. He was caring and kind and corrected me in a very loving way. I experienced healing and a sense of being greatly valued. I no longer felt worthless.

Jesus demonstrated great love for people, especially the outcast and unpopular. He refused to condemn the woman caught in adultery. He searched out the demon-possessed. Jesus brought light to the darkness; and he calls us to be people of light who bring healing, love and acceptance to others.

Prayer: *Dear God, may we be filled with your love so that it flows from us to those in need. We pray in the name of Jesus, who taught us to call you Father, saying, 'Our Father in heaven, hallowed be your name, your kingdom come, your will be done, on earth as it is in heaven. Give us today our daily bread. And forgive us our debts, as we also have forgiven our debtors. And lead us not into temptation, but deliver us from the evil one.'* Amen*

Thought for the day: God brings healing and restoration.

Sue Bond (Western Australia, Australia)

PRAYER FOCUS: CHILDREN OF PARENTS WHO SHOW FAVOURITISM   53
* Matthew 6:9–13 (NIV)

'Let God Bless You'

Read 2 Corinthians 9:6–15

This service that you perform is not only supplying the needs of the Lord's people but is also overflowing in many expressions of thanks to God.
2 Corinthians 9:12 (NIV)

Late the other night, standing on the railway platform waiting for a train, I was approached by a homeless man. With no sign of a train approaching, I turned an ear to hear his story—the same story I had heard from many who live on the streets of our city: drugs, crime, the loss of a loved one and a life in disarray. He was just looking for some food. We had a light moment laughing about our favourite sports teams, and I felt moved to help him. As the train approached, I handed him more money than he might usually see, knowing it was enough to get him into safe, clean lodging around the corner. He was shocked by the gift, and I was shocked at the phrase that came from my lips: 'Let God bless you.'

As the train pulled away, the meaning of that moment hit me. In that instant, God had brought two paths together—one where a blessing was needed and one where many blessings had already been given. I am incredibly thankful for the blessings of my life. But in that moment, I could see that I had been blessed to be a blessing, just as Paul had told the Christians in Corinth.

Faith turns our hearts to God for blessing in our most dire moments. But that same faith can lead us to approach life with open eyes and open hearts to bless others.

Prayer: *O God, giver of all good, use us to convey your blessing to our brothers and sisters. Amen*

Thought for the day: God's blessings should reach beyond us to others.

Robert T. Rupp (Illinois, US)

Freely Receive, Freely Give

Read Ephesians 2:1–10

By grace you have been saved through faith, and this is not your own doing; it is the gift of God.
Ephesians 2:8 (NRSV)

'There's no such thing as a free lunch!' I often hear this common expression in my daily life. Because I grew up in a society based on merit, I was taught to work for what I want to achieve. Study diligently at school, work hard for high wages and dress to impress were some of the expectations set before me. Yet our Father in heaven offers a totally different standard. God freely gives us the best gift in this world—God's Son, Christ Jesus.

People like me, and perhaps like you, who were taught to earn and not merely receive, have a tendency to try to earn everything—including our salvation. We may think that we need to be good, kind, pleasant and charitable people. Yes, we may be good people according to this world's standard. But one sin makes us sinners, and so we can never be good enough. Even so, God loves us and wants to be in relationship with us. God gave his one Son to make all of us sons and daughters.

Prayer: *Dear God, thank you for your grace that saves us. As we freely receive it, let us freely give by praying for and serving others. Amen*

Thought for the day: I can offer the gift of Christ to someone today.

Steffanie Berlian Simatupang (Jakarta, Indonesia)

Herb's Bucket

Read Matthew 25:14–30

To all those who have, more will be given, and they will have an abundance; but from those who have nothing, even what they have will be taken away.
Matthew 25:29 (NRSV)

When my husband and I moved into our house, we noticed a wonderful garden next door filled with beautiful flowers and wholesome vegetables. Our neighbour, Herb, was a master gardener. But more than that, he was generous. Herb hung a bucket on our side of the fence that separated our back garden. As he quietly worked in his garden, Herb would fill our bucket with wonderful things. One day it might be tomatoes; the next day, potatoes. Another day it was cucumbers; and the day after, fresh beetroot. We never saw Herb filling our bucket, but the evidence of his presence was undeniable.

One day as I emptied that bucket, I thought about what would happen if I forgot that it was there or perhaps became too lazy to empty it. The vegetables would rot and be wasted.

Maybe God is like Herb… working quietly in the garden of our lives, filling our 'buckets' with gifts and skills for us to use. Has God given you a gift that you are not using? When we use what is in our buckets, God can fill them up again.

Prayer: *Dear God, help us to discern and to fully use the talents, skills and gifts you give us, to bring you glory. Amen*

Thought for the day: What has God put in my 'bucket'?

Link2Life: *Is there a neighbour who needs your practical help today?*

Glenys Nellist (Michigan, US)

Move It!

Read James 1:19–24
This is love, that we walk according to his commandments.
2 John 6 (NRSV)

I am not a frequent flyer, so I was unfamiliar with the 'people-mover' contraption at the airport. Stepping on to the large human-conveyor belt, I relaxed as I it carried me across the airport. Then, without warning, the machine stopped. Conversations hushed. We all stood, waiting to start moving again. Finally, someone behind me said, 'Walk!' Somehow that idea had not occurred to us. As the person in front got the message, we all began to move forward again—the old-fashioned way.

Sometimes the church is like that moving pavement. Saved by God's grace, we find a fellowship of like-minded people. But sadly many times we do not move forward. Only as each member exercises his or her gifts can we together make progress, serving the world that Christ died to save.

The urgent word of that airport traveller is the same one our Saviour utters to every Christian. To us—when we are paralysed by a status-quo, stand-still mentality—Christ says, 'Walk!'

Prayer: *Dear Lord, move us to take personal responsibility and to progress toward being the people you want us to be. Amen*

Thought for the day: Am I an obstacle in God's path, or am I walking in the way of Christ?

Thomas Buice (Tennessee, US)

Riding the Waves

Read Mark 6:45–51

Mightier than the thunder of the great waters, mightier than the breakers of the sea—the Lord on high is mighty.
Psalm 93:4 (NIV)

During our annual family trip to the beach, our children were learning to swim in the waves. We showed them how to jump at the right time and how to turn away from a wave that was too big or that broke at the wrong time. Most important, we taught them to answer the question, 'Are you OK?' After lots of jumps and splashes and a few mouthfuls of ocean, they gained confidence and began to enjoy the water.

As I watched my children play in the surf, I began to see that riding the waves is like steering through life. Our lives are unpredictable. The swell that looks menacing from far off may be a mere ripple by the time it arrives. The wave that passes me by may knock down my neighbour. We cannot predict the hard or easy times; we cannot be prepared for every eventuality.

Yet I also realise that God sees our struggles and is with us even when the world knocks us down. No matter how difficult the waters, we are never out of God's sight. We can remember the mighty Lord who made the seas we navigate.

Prayer: *Dear God of land and sea, comfort us with your strength and your love whenever we feel afraid. Remind us that you teach and guide us by your mighty hand. Amen*

Thought for the day: God's strength is greater than anything that knocks us down.

Nancy A. Johnson (Georgia, US)

Fulfilling the Law

Read Matthew 5:17–20

Jesus said, 'Think not that I am come to destroy the law, or the prophets: I am not come to destroy, but to fulfil.'
Matthew 5:17 (KJV)

The people I work with in the foreign-language department of a university all communicate in English, though not always the same English. We argue so much about British and American English that I sometimes start to wonder if it is the same language at all.

The other day, instead of wading into the debate, I found myself thinking of Matthew 5:17. The passage seems straightforward enough: the old laws would stand. But Jesus might have been saying that he wasn't as concerned about the law as about people's actions.

In my work, we get caught up in the interpretation of words and phrases. What is more important is the substance of the documents. In our religious lives, we can become engrossed in the small details and nuances of Bible passages. What is more important is the life we are supposed to live.

Maybe when Jesus talked about fulfilling the law, he was talking about living according to its deeper meaning. His message of compassion, peace and understanding and his life show us how to live.

Next time an argument breaks out among my colleagues, I'll try to bring them back to the importance of what we are writing. And in my spiritual life, I will spend less time focusing on the nuances of Bible passages. Instead, I am going to focus on living as Jesus did.

Prayer: *Dear God, teach us to live according to what is truly important, bringing life and healing as Jesus did. Amen*

Thought for the day: What does the Bible mean for my life?

Christopher McKenna (South Lanarkshire, Scotland)

PRAYER FOCUS: THOSE WHO ARGUE ABOUT THE BIBLE

Reflections

Read Exodus 34:29–35

We all, who with unveiled faces contemplate the Lord's glory, are being transformed into his image with ever-increasing glory, which comes from the Lord, who is the Spirit.
2 Corinthians 3:18 (NIV)

Last year my husband and I took a Bible study class together to incorporate the Bible into our daily lives, to better serve as disciples of Christ. I was inspired by the story of Moses who came down the mountain after being in God's presence, unaware that his face was radiant. How awesome to experience God's glory so much so that others could witness its impact on me just by being in my presence!

As I thought about it, I realised that I have experienced God's presence. I've seen his face in my family members. I've heard his voice in words of love and compassion spoken to me in times of stress. I've felt his glory while viewing the beauty of the world. When I look back on my life, I see that his hand guided me to become a teacher.

I have experienced God. So I ask myself, Can others see God reflected in my face, or do I wear a 'veil', hiding God? I am afraid others too often see a veil. Realising this has made me consciously try harder to reflect God's love to others, including strangers I see in passing. As we reflect God's glory, we are being transformed into his likeness.

Prayer: *Dear heavenly Father, thank you for forgiving us and for showering us with blessings and guiding us into your service. Help us to share your love with others. Amen*

Thought for the day: How can I more faithfully reflect God to those around me?

Marilyn Walker (Virginia, US)

See the Whole

Read Psalm 103:1–14

As a father has compassion on his children, so the Lord has compassion on those who fear him; for he knows how we are formed, he remembers that we are dust.
Psalm 103:13–14 (NIV)

My mother committed suicide when I was six years old. I found her body. No one spoke to me about her after her death, so I grew up not knowing her as a whole person. I remembered her most vividly at her worst moment.

On the 50th anniversary of her death, the Lord nudged me to get to know my mother. In response, I spent six months researching her life and travelling to places where she had lived, studied and worked. With the support of my wife, my dad and many other people, I was able to 'meet' my mother. I learned about her life and how much she loved me. Instead of a distant, unknown and traumatic figure, she became my mum.

During this healing process, God showed me that as I strive to see others in the way he views them, I must see beyond their worst moments. Jesus did not reduce Peter to the lack of faith Peter revealed when he sank beneath the waves or when he denied his Lord. Instead, Jesus saw Peter as a flawed follower who loved him deeply and who had gifts that transcended his sins.

We can extend the same healing grace to those around us and to those who have come before us.

Prayer: *Dear Lord, help us as we seek to extend your grace to family members who have hurt us. Amen*

Thought for the day: In God's sight, our worst moments do not define us.

Steve Messer (Indiana, US)

PRAYER FOCUS: FAMILIES OF SUICIDE VICTIMS

Pass It On!

Read Romans 10:11–18

How are they to believe in one of whom they have never heard? And how are they to hear without someone to proclaim him?
Romans 10:14 (NRSV)

I normally read *The Upper Room* online at my computer each morning. I hadn't seen a paper copy in years until my husband spotted an issue of it lying on a bench in the porch of a restaurant one Sunday afternoon. Apparently someone had left it behind after receiving it at church. Fearing that the restaurant staff might throw the magazine away, we decided to pick it up and take it home.

Finding the magazine the way that we did made me wonder how many copies of *The Upper Room* are taken to nursing homes, hospitals, schools and the homes of invalids. How many are sent to prisons? Since *The Upper Room* is published in 40 languages and is a convenient size, I imagine that many copies cross national borders and travel to remote locations to be received thankfully. And a few sit on benches waiting for someone to pick them up and say, 'I haven't seen one of these in years!' Then they put it in their pockets or bags to go into homes, perhaps to be read aloud to others and to touch more hearts. God's message of love and grace nurtures everyone it reaches, wherever it goes.

Prayer: *Dear heavenly Father, thank you for those who help us follow Christ more faithfully. We pray for all those yearning for Christian community. Amen*

Thought for the day: Whether we are alone or in a group, when we use *The Upper Room* we are part of a worldwide community praying together.

Mary Hunt Webb (New Mexico, US)

Poured Out, Poured In

Read 1 Samuel 1:1–18

Trust in him at all times, you people; pour out your hearts to him, for God is our refuge.
Psalm 62:8 (NIV)

Hannah came to the temple and poured out her misery and troubles to the Lord. She was without a child but her husband's other wife had children, and she never let Hannah forget it. How vigorously did Hannah pour out her troubles to God? Observing her, Eli, the priest, thought she was drunk and chastised her. Hannah let him know otherwise, and he told her to go in peace.

When we open our hearts to God the way Hannah did, everything in us that has held us captive can pour out. As we let go of this, the Holy Spirit cares gently for us, helping us to rest in God, our true refuge. We find hope, 'And hope does not disappoint us because God's love has been poured into our hearts through the Holy Spirit that has been given to us' (Romans 5:5, NRSV).

When we pour out our misery, trials and fears to God, we will be wrapped in grace. God pours love into our hearts and brings us healing.

Prayer: *Holy God, may we never lose faith in your healing power. Fill us, we pray, with your blessed hope. Amen*

Thought for the day: When we pour out our troubles to God, he pours hope and peace into us.

John Eyberg (Oklahoma, US)

True Value

Read Psalm 119:33–40

'Let not the wise boast of their wisdom or the strong boast of their strength or the rich boast of their riches, but let the one who boasts boast about this: that they have the understanding to know me, that I am the Lord, who exercises kindness, justice and righteousness on earth, for in these I delight,' declares the Lord.
Jeremiah 9:23–24 (NIV)

I am privileged to work with remarkable people in a workplace that is largely focused on academic reward. Yet this highly intellectual environment brings the risk of allowing academic achievement to become the measuring stick of a person's worth.

Adopting such a value system is easy. Society often measures our worth by our success, knowledge or wealth. But what are these achievements if they are not attained while seeking after God and his purposes? Does any of them make us more important in the Lord's eyes? No.

God loves us unconditionally. Reading Jeremiah 9:23–24, we see that strength, riches and wisdom are not negatives. But first and foremost, God longs for us to be people who devote ourselves to seeking him and understanding his ways.

Prayer: *Dear Lord, thank you that our value is not determined by our riches, strength or intellect, but by your unchanging love for us. May we diligently seek to know and honour you, remembering that our hearts, not our achievements, are most important to you. Amen*

Thought for the day: Consider your value from God's perspective.

Adele Jones (Queensland, Australia)

Firmly Grounded

Read Ephesians 3:16–21

It is for freedom that Christ has set us free. Stand firm, then, and do not let yourselves be burdened again by a yoke of slavery.
Galatians 5:1 (NIV)

The rotary clothes dryer was fixed on a gravelled shelf at the end of the garden, where it would catch the breeze and any sunlight.

My sister was recovering from an operation and I offered to hang out the washing. Placing the basket on the ground I attempted to open the umbrella-like dryer. To my horror, the central post lifted right out of its metal socket. A shower of small stones and gravel poured into the hole, making it impossible to replace the post. It took me about ten minutes on my knees to remove the stones blocking the socket and prevent more from sliding in. Only then could the post be settled back and firmly grounded, allowing the plastic lines of the dryer to open correctly. Soon the clothes were blowing in the breeze and my sister and I were chuckling at my mistake.

When I think about 'being rooted and grounded in love', I realise that Christ's love is as solid as that metal socket. If I am somehow unsteadied or knocked off balance, allowing things to come between me and him, I cannot stand tall and feel the wind of his Spirit moving in my life. The solution is to get on my knees and ask him to remove the blockage.

Prayer: *Lord, thank you for the strength and security of your love. Please deal with any prejudice or sin that affects my relationship with you. Amen*

Thought for the day: Christ wants to fill me with his love.

Barbara Collier (Cumbria, England)

Confidence in God

Read Exodus 3:7–12

The Lord said, 'I've clearly seen my people oppressed in Egypt. I've heard their cry of injustice because of their slave masters. I know about their pain.'
Exodus 3:7 (CEB)

Our baby has suffered from severe eczema since he was about three months old, and it has been difficult to see him live with such an irritating and often painful condition. At times when the inflammation and itchiness of his skin are so agonising that he looks at his father and me with tear-filled eyes, all we want to do is hold him close and let him know that we hear his cries. We want him to know we understand that he is in pain and that we are doing all we possibly can to alleviate it. This experience has given me a new perspective on the love of God.

We all go through seasons of life that are especially difficult and painful. In those times I find indescribable reassurance in knowing that just as God heard the cries of the Israelites and knew about their pain as captives in Egypt, he hears our cries of pain, frustration and desperation. Not only does God hear us and know us, he wants to bring us comfort and peace.

Prayer: *God of all comfort, help us to remember when we feel alone and forgotten that you hear our cries, see our pain, and are working to bring us peace. Show us how to trust you even when our faith seems small, as we pray, 'Father, hallowed be your name, your kingdom come. Give us each day our daily bread. Forgive us our sins, for we also forgive everyone who sins against us. And lead us not into temptation.'* Amen*

Thought for the day: God's ears are tuned to our cries.

Shannon L. Brophy (Texas, US)

* Luke 11:2–4 (NIV)

A Daily Reality

Read 1 Peter 1:3–9

Although you have not seen him, you love him; and even though you do not see him now, you believe in him and rejoice with an indescribable and glorious joy, for you are receiving the outcome of your faith, the salvation of your souls.
1 Peter 1:8–9 (NRSV)

There's no doubt about it—I enjoy rock concerts! They're announced well in advance; we book our seats; and as the day draws near, the anticipation grows. These events can serve as a wonderful stress reliever as they allow us to lose a few inhibitions. For a few hours we can sing loudly, dance in the aisles and generally have a good time with the music we love. The music and the event itself often remain in our memories for weeks.

Is the season of Easter a bit like a rock concert in your life? Do we sing loudly and uninhibitedly dance with joy at the amazing gift that God, through Christ Jesus, offers each of us? Is it our favourite season? How long do we remember Easter once we move into the next period of calendar time?

Every Sunday is meant to be a mini-Easter for each of us. We intentionally try to recreate the same joy and thankfulness during Sunday worship each week so we can carry this event into every day. Our joy can be a witness to the life Christ offers all of us—and that we are meant to offer others. That way Easter can be a daily reality, not just a memory.

Prayer: *Loving God, thank you for salvation through Christ's sacrifice and resurrection. Teach us to live in joy each day as we remember the reality of Easter. Amen*

Thought for the day: Celebrate the joy of Christ's resurrection each and every day!

Roland Rink (Gauteng, South Africa)

Breath Prayer

Breath holds an amazing power. It feels soft and delicate—but think about how it announces that we are alive when we enter the world and how we die when our breath expires. It's so much a part of us that usually we breathe without even being aware of it. And the closeness of each breath is rivalled only by how close God is to us. We are created with the *ruach* (Hebrew for breath, spirit) of God entering our bodies (Genesis 2:7; Job 27:3). So our breaths are in constant relationship with our Creator. Each breath is a reminder of God with us and within us.

When I first started running, I became amazingly aware of my breath. I felt the power of each inhale and exhale, especially when I was short of breath or when maintaining my breath up a steep hill. I suddenly felt the pull, release and tension of breath.

And in these daily runs, I discover the discipline of breath prayer. As my body performs one of its most natural functions—breathing—I learn to quiet all that is within me and hear only my breath's paraphrase of John 3:30: 'More of you, Lord,' on each inhale. 'Less of me,' on each exhale. Breath prayer can serve as a simple way to journey toward ceaseless prayer (Romans 12:12). We are always breathing for as long as we are alive. When we attach the discipline of prayer to our breaths, we, too, can find ourselves constantly in the presence of God.

Breath prayer is simple prayer. At first it may feel very different to pay so much attention to the breath and repeat the same phrase. We often are more accustomed to wordier prayers, but breath prayers are a meditation that can silence us enough to hear God's voice and feel his presence.

We know so much about staying busy and being entertained in this world of ours—the infinite scheduling, the constant demands, the steady images and ads and Tweets being tossed in our direction. We sometimes even treat our time with God as if it's something to check off our lists. According to a study in 2011, about 39 per cent of the participating self-identified Christians performed three 'normal' religious activities such as attending church, Bible study and praying during the week of the study. When it came to more contemplative practices of silence, solitude and meditation, however, these were practised quite infrequently.[1]

Tuning ourselves to our breath requires intention, release of busyness and pushing through discomfort sometimes. The beauty of the breath prayer, however, is the acceptance of that very tension. When praying it, we don't seek to be perfect or pretend that we aren't busy and constantly pulled away from Christ in this world. This prayer is the very place to confess this reality and ask for a change. Part of what makes this simple prayer method so powerful is its honesty. In the parable of the Pharisee and the tax collector, we see in the tax collector's simple breath prayer, 'God, have mercy on me, a sinner' (Luke 18:10–13, NIV), a simple statement recognising how great God is and how much we need his greatness.

We start by addressing God during our inhale. For my run, the entire inhale is an address and request—'More of you, Lord'— because I desire to inhale more of God's grace, love and mercy. The inhale can also be drawing simply on your chosen name for God, such as 'Christ, the Son of the living God' (Matthew 16:16, CEB), or 'Lamb of God, who takes away the sin of the world' (John 1:29). With the many possible combinations, the inhaling statement can be as long or as short as our breaths will allow. Whatever phrase we choose must simply be authentic to our relationship with God in that very moment we are breathing. Our exhaled statement is something we want to release to God. This may be in the form of a request like, 'have mercy on me, a sinner'; an offering like, 'I give my life to you' or a statement of thanksgiving like, 'you are worthy of praise'. Or the prayer can be very unique and unstructured. The full expression of the breath prayer may look like this:

1. barna.org/faith-spirituality/524-self-described-christians-dominate-america-but-wrestle-with-four-aspects-of-spiritual-depth?q=prayer

Inhale	Exhale
Lamb of God,	
who takes away the sins of the world,	have mercy on me, a sinner.
Heavenly Creator,	forgive me, I pray.
You are the potter;	I am the clay.
Lord, Jesus Christ, I believe	help my unbelief!
Gracious God, giver of life	thank you for each breath.
Poured in…	poured out.

This prayer can be practised in a quiet, still place or while exercising, doing the washing up, driving—wherever!

Several meditations in this issue deal with prayer and meditation, honest humility and developing a more intimate relationship with Christ. Consider reading the following meditations again as you reflect: May 2, 6, 8, 13, 21, 22, 23, June 4, 6, 23, 26, July 3 and 15, and August 2 and 10.

Questions for Reflection:

1. Have you ever had a loss or obstruction of breath? What does that feel like? If God is our breath of life, what does it feel like when we lose communication with him?

2. Consider when you have felt closest to God. How did you experience him during this time?

3. Write this down. Now consider your heart's deepest desires, and write them down. Reflect on what you've written, and create a breath prayer from it.

4. What does prayer mean for you? Which scripture texts have taught you about prayer?

5. Consider the honesty of the tax collector in Luke 18:13. Why is it important to practise honesty in all of life and especially in prayer?

Ciona D. Rouse lives in Nashville where she loves God, writes, practises yoga and enjoys the fullness of life and the gift of every breath.

Where Are You?

Read Matthew 19:10–14

Which one of you, having a hundred sheep and losing one of them, does not leave the ninety-nine in the wilderness and go after the one that is lost until he finds it?
Luke 15:4 (NRSV)

When I began my first appointment as a pastor, we moved into the parsonage with our three cats and Maggie—a fun-loving, tail-wagging Basset with lots of energy. Two parishioners and I set to building a dog run and put Maggie inside to let her get acquainted with her new home. After an hour or two, I decided to go out and check on her. I panicked when I saw that Maggie was gone. Our family was worried because a main road was very close. I could see in my mind's eye her poor lifeless body. We got into the truck and drove all over, looking for her and calling her name.

We found her exploring a neighbour's garden. When she saw me, she started running toward me. What a reunion—wagging, barking, jumping, running around in circles—and Maggie was happy too. It was like the biggest party you could imagine. What a celebration! My Maggie who was lost was now found!

That's the way God searches for us. From the very beginning we see that it is not the person who goes searching for God but God who goes searching for the person. The whole Bible is a story of God searching for us until our relationship was restored in Christ.

Prayer: *Watchful and caring God, thank you for searching for us and providing a way back home. Amen*

Thought for the day: When we are lost, God searches for us and brings us home.

Michael Morelan (Alabama, US)

Bearing Fruit

Read Mark 11:12–24

Jesus said, 'I am the true vine… Remain in me, as I also remain in you. No branch can bear fruit by itself; it must remain in the vine. Neither can you bear fruit unless you remain in me.'
John 15:1, 4 (NIV)

My fig tree had yielded fruit for the first time. Although there was not much of it, I was still excited and happy about my discovery. For several years, when my fig tree should have been bearing fruit, it produced only leaves.

Just as Jesus was not pleased when the fig tree mentioned in the scripture reading did not bear fruit, I was also disappointed about my fruitless tree. However, success came when I placed the tree in a spot where it got more sun. In addition, I prayed for the tree to bear fruit, remembering that Jesus advised his disciples, 'Have faith in God… whatever you ask for in prayer, believe that you have received it, and it will be yours' (Mark 11:22, 24).

Of course, when it comes to bearing fruit in our service to God, faith is the key factor. Jesus described how we can faithfully bear fruit in today's reading: 'If you remain in me and I in you, you will bear much fruit' (John 15:5). My fig tree may or may not bear more fruit next year. However, by faithfully serving God, each of us can bear fruit every single day!

Prayer: *Sustainer of life, make us ready and willing to bear more of your fruit. Amen*

Thought for the day: Our faith in God helps us bear fruit all year long.

Jimmie Oliver Fleming (Virginia, US)

Pray without Ceasing

Read Philippians 4:4–9

Do not be anxious about anything, but in everything, by prayer and petition, with thanksgiving, present your requests to God.
Philippians 4:6 (NIV)

In our women's Bible study group, some members explained that they have a regular, quiet time for meditating, reading the Bible, and speaking and listening to God. One of our group explained that she didn't have a structured quiet time but spoke to God on and off throughout the day. But method is not important. What matters is communicating with our Creator. We would not ignore a human friend; why would we ignore God?

1 Thessalonians says, 'Pray continually' (5:17). How do we do that? We can pray as soon as we wake up in the morning and thank God for another day to praise and to serve. When at home we can pray for our family and loved ones. At work we can pray for our colleagues, our bosses and the business.

Travelling also brings opportunities to pray—for those we sit by on the train or bus. Travelling by car, we can pray for other drivers and for the safety of all who are on the road. When walking, we can pray for those we see and for the families in the houses we pass. Travelling by air gives us an opportunity to pray for the places we are visiting or flying over. Prayer can be as natural and continual as breathing.

Prayer: *Dear Lord, we give thanks that you hear our prayers—whenever and wherever we offer them. Amen*

Thought for the day: Every hour offers opportunities to pray.

Link2Life: *Whatever you are doing today, stop and pray.*

Carol Purves (Cumbria, England)

From Setback to Comeback

Read Joel 2:28–32

If the Spirit of him who raised Jesus from the dead dwells in you, he who raised Christ from the dead will give life to your mortal bodies also through his Spirit that dwells in you.
Romans 8:11 (NRSV)

Sometimes in life we may face major setbacks such as health issues, financial issues, emotional struggles or the loss of a job. When these setbacks occur we can feel vulnerable, scared, upset and even angry. When I suddenly lost my job and had no form of income for my family of four and all the bills kept coming in, I had a range of emotions. I was scared, uncertain, angry and bitter.

I wonder if the people who lived in the time of Jesus and witnessed his death felt similar emotions. I wonder if they actually thought he would rise again in three days.

Perhaps one lesson the crucifixion, death and resurrection of Christ illustrates is how a monumental setback can initiate a monumental comeback.

I realised that the Spirit given to us following the most historic comeback in history also lives in us as believers and is interceding on our behalf.

Prayer: *Dear God, help us to see you in all circumstances. When we face tough situations, help us to remember that the Holy Spirit is living and working in us as we pray, 'Father, hallowed be your name, your kingdom come. Give us each day our daily bread. Forgive us our sins, for we also forgive everyone who sins against us. And lead us not into temptation.'* Amen*

Thought for the day: God can turn setbacks into comebacks.

Brad Richardson (Georgia, US)

PRAYER FOCUS: SOMEONE FACING A SETBACK
* Luke 11:2–4 (NIV)

Trust

Read Proverbs 3:1–6

Honour your father and your mother, so that you may live long in the land the Lord your God is giving you.
Exodus 20:12 (NIV)

My parents live in Florida. As they get older, they are no longer able to enjoy the nice weather and the visits to the beach. Over the last four years, they have experienced many health concerns, including diabetes, cancer, heart disease and arthritis. After the last hospital stay, I asked them to move to my home to live with me.

When I telephoned them, my dad broke down and cried. 'I'm scared,' he said. 'How are we going to move? We're old, sick and have no money.'

I said, 'Dad, do you trust me?'

'Well, of course I trust you.'

When I got off the phone, I realised the commitment I had made. I felt as if their well-being were totally in my hands. I would need to sell their home, make travel arrangements, make appointments with doctors, make my home wheelchair-friendly, and then take on the important role of caring for them. I am single and own a business. 'How can I take on any more responsibilities?' I thought. Now, I was the one who was scared.

I cried out to God for strength and support. Then I remembered the question I'd asked my dad. When we are scared and don't know what to do or what the future holds, God asks, 'Do you trust me?' God had answered my prayers before I asked.

Prayer: *Dear God, source of strength, when we are afraid, give us faith to trust in you. Amen*

Thought for the day: By honouring our parents, we honour God's command.

Karen Bryant Wood (Indiana, US)

No Higher Love

Read Romans 8:31–39

As high as the heavens are above the earth, so great is his love for those who fear him; as far as the east is from the west, so far has he removed our transgressions from us.
Psalm 103:11–12 (NIV)

As a little girl on my swing, I tried to touch the sky with my toes. But no matter how high I sailed, I could never reach it. The sky seemed unfathomably high.

In my teens, I experienced my first plane ride. I was flying through the same sky I'd thought was untouchable. With clouds for company, I couldn't imagine anything higher. But I knew that beyond the clouds were planets, constellations and the moon. Could anything be higher?

Beyond the bright blue sky I tried to touch with my toes, past the height of clouds I'd experienced as a teenager, and beyond even the stars in outer space, the love of God reaches farther still. Our Lord is called the 'Most High' for a reason: No love is more expansive. When I became a Christian, I learned that God's love reaches beyond my mistakes, my fears and my sin.

Tonight, take a close look at the stars. If you can't imagine anything higher, remember that God's love stretches farther.

Prayer: *Dear God, let us understand the depth and height of your love. Help us to accept and experience your love today and to love you in return. Amen*

Thought for the day: The rich love of God has no boundaries.

Elizabeth Veldboom (Colorado, US)

Present in the Storms

Read Mark 4:35–41

Jesus said, 'Go and make disciples of all the nations... teaching them to obey everything I have commanded you. And surely I am with you always, to the very end of the age.'
Matthew 28:19–20 (NIV)

Lightning dashed across the sky and struck the ground in front and behind us. The rains soaked us as we struggled along the hilly and rocky five-mile path. Drenched in the non-stop downpour, we sang and prayed.

Our church had decided to obey the great commission by preaching God's word to one of the villages across the hill. We were returning from this evangelistic journey, bursting with joy at the way the Lord had opened the hearts of the people. Then suddenly, our elation turned into fear and apprehension when the dreaded storm began to pound us.

'Didn't the Lord promise to be with us until the end of the age?' I asked myself. 'Why is God allowing our lives to be threatened by this storm when we are taking the gospel to the lost?' As these thoughts dashed through my mind, the part of the message in the great commission that says, 'I am with you always, to the very end of the age' expanded in meaning for me.

I realised that God's promise to be with us until the end of the age does not guarantee that there will be no difficulties as we proclaim the message. But, in the midst of the storm, our Lord is there with us.

Prayer: *Dear Lord, help us to remember your promise to be with us— even in the storm. Amen*

Thought for the day: The storms in our lives can help us see God's promise to be with us.

Francis Lawer Sackitey (Eastern Region, Ghana)

The Bridge

Read Romans 6:4–11

God made him who had no sin to be sin for us, so that in him we might become the righteousness of God.

2 Corinthians 5:21 (NIV)

I watch the swift, smooth, swollen Mississippi River as it glides by. Just below the surface, deep, roiling currents tug and push. As I gaze across the river, I contemplate what would be required to ford such a monstrous body of water on my own. With no tools at hand, with no instructions, without a bridge—how could I presume to get across this huge, murky divide? By my own efforts, it would simply be impossible.

While I watch the river, I think about how swiftly my life is coursing by. Underneath the illusion of a smooth surface, emotional currents of ego and pride tug at me. Just as I cannot fathom swimming alone across the river, I cannot grasp any means by which I can reach heaven on my own. How can I ever stand before God without tools, without instructions, without a bridge? Through my own efforts, I cannot. No one can.

Thankfully, God provided the way and built a bridge to heaven and everlasting life through his son, Jesus Christ. This bridge was made possible by way of a great sacrifice and glorious resurrection. Jesus is the bridge that crosses the great divide between us and eternity. We must simply believe to receive salvation.

Prayer: *Dear God, thank you for offering a way to spend eternity with you. Teach us to love and serve you each day of our lives. Amen*

Thought for the day: Christ's resurrection provides us a bridge to salvation.

Mary Hughes (Missouri, US)

How Well are we Listening?

Read Matthew 7:24–27
Then Samuel said, 'Speak, for your servant is listening.'
1 Samuel 3:10 (NIV)

I like to read the newspaper each evening. It helps me to keep abreast of what is happening in the world, and to relax at the end of a busy day. I often sit in the living-room where my wife watches TV and my son is on his computer, and there is noise all around. Then I become aware of my wife's voice saying, 'Dear, are you listening to me?'

The problem is that, while reading the paper, I may have been aware that she was speaking to me but I was not concentrating enough to hear, understand or act on what she was saying.

How often we fail to hear God in the same way! He will try to speak to us through his word or through prayer, both during our busy day and during our quiet times, but we let his voice be crowded out by our activities or other distractions.

Jesus often said that whoever had ears, should hear. I am still working on it: but how important it is that we set aside time to allow God to speak into our lives, to concentrate, to listen to his voice and be ready to do his will.

Prayer: *Father God, help me to set aside time today to listen when you speak to me. Amen*

Thought for the day: God wants to speak to me: am I willing to listen?

Mark A. Wallace (Suffolk, England)

WWJRD?

Read Acts 4:23–31

The wicked flee when no one pursues, but the righteous are as bold as a lion.
Proverbs 28:1 (NRSV)

A few years ago the acronym WWJD referred to a popular phrase—'What Would Jesus Do?' Until recently, I had a great misunderstanding about what those initials stood for. I thought when I was the nice girl who went to church and turned the other way when people offended me that I was being like Jesus. It is true that there are times when we must 'turn the other cheek' (see Matthew 5:39). However, as I have come to know Jesus more fully through God's word, I found Jesus to be a bold and courageous man who did not back down from confrontation and was not afraid of speaking the truth in love (see Ephesians 4:15) even if it offended people. I began to ask myself, WWJRD—What Would Jesus Really Do?

As I looked to the people who followed Christ, I discovered men and women who were not afraid to stand boldly for Christ and all he taught. As I became more bold and courageous in my Christian walk, I found true freedom. Too often, Christians in the Church think that being a nice person is the way to be like Christ. However, when we see a fuller picture of Jesus through studying scripture, we can learn from him and find courage and boldness to stand for him. The truth of God's word will set us free to be the people he created us to be and to find true peace and confidence through Christ.

Prayer: *Dear heavenly Father, help us to know Jesus and what he stood for. Give us the strength and courage to stand boldly for your kingdom. In Jesus' name we pray. Amen*

Thought for the day: We can get to know the real Jesus by reading the Bible every day.

Jodi Wheeler (Arizona, US)

A Grateful Parting

Read Philippians 1:3–11
This is the day that the Lord has made; let us rejoice and be glad in it.
Psalm 118:24 (NRSV)

My sons and I spent a week's holiday with my father. However, I soon became sad when I realised that there were only a few days left before we would have to leave him to go home.

Early one morning, I heard my father singing: 'This is the day that the Lord has made; we will rejoice and be glad in it.' While I listened to his faithful words of grateful thanksgiving, I was reminded that God does not want our joy to be diminished.

On the day we prepared to leave, my father offered a prayer. His words calmed me. 'Dear God, thank you for this visit. Help us to have grateful hearts for the time we have together.'

Too often we worry about what's ahead. Or we sometimes hurry through our lives and forget that God creates purpose in the heart of each moment. When we are open to the Holy Spirit's working in our lives, God can guide us and provide opportunities for us to recognise when we have been blessed. Then, he can reward us with a grateful heart as we learn to trust and obey our Creator.

Prayer: *Dear heavenly Father, thank you for moments we share with those we love who live far away. Help us to feel your peace when it's time to leave them and allow us to live with gratitude. Amen*

Thought for the day: God can help us to embrace each moment with grateful hearts.

Nancy Grachek Hodges (Illinois, US)

Give it Away

Read 1 Timothy 6:17–19

Heal the sick, raise the dead, cleanse those who have leprosy, drive out demons. Freely you have received; freely give.
Matthew 10:8 (NIV)

The phone rang late one night after I had already gone to bed. It was my friend, Jim, who said, 'I'm sorry for calling so late, but I just had to give you something.'

'Give me something?' I replied.

He explained that he had recently promised himself—and God— that he would give away something every day that year. 'It doesn't have to be much,' he said. 'I've given some money to a kid who lost his money in a sweets machine, or a book I've enjoyed to someone I think will like it. But I realised a few minutes ago that I hadn't given anything away yet today, so I thought I'd ring you.'

'What are you going to give me over the phone?' I asked.

'It may not be much,' he answered, 'but it's something.' He then proceeded to read me a short poem that expressed his deep love and respect for me. It was truly a gift.

Imagine giving something away every day for a year—or even for a month or a week! It may seem incredible, but it's not impossible—as my friend's late-night phone call proves! Such generosity can bless the one who gives, even as it blesses those who receive.

Prayer: *Dear gracious God, make me a channel of your blessing to someone today. Amen*

Thought for the day: As God gives to me, so I can give to others.

Robert R. Hostetler (Ohio, US)

Never without Hope

Read Romans 8:18–25
May the God of hope fill you with all joy and peace in believing, so that you may abound in hope by the power of the Holy Spirit.
Romans 15:13 (NRSV)

In my work as a nurse, I visit patients in their homes. Two years ago, in the summer, I went to a home in which both mother and son were terminally ill. They knew that they would never get better, but in this wonderfully bright home I was met with kindness and smiles. We talked and laughed for a long time. There were no sad faces there; instead there was hope. The son could no longer get out of bed; he was 19 years old and could hardly move his hands and feet. Yet from his sick bed, he was taking school exams and dreamed of going to college.

He died late one Sunday evening at the end of October. It was cold outside. When he took his last breath, a butterfly appeared in the room. I was really surprised to see it; after all, you don't normally see butterflies in the autumn. The butterfly reminded me that even in the most difficult moments we have hope. When he died, his textbooks still lay on the bedside table. He had continued hoping to get better and to go to college.

Six weeks later his mother died. I no longer go to that home; but every time I walk past it or see a butterfly, my heart is filled with hope and gratitude for God's gift of love and eternal life.

Prayer: *Dear God, help us never to lose hope but to trust in you for ever. Amen*

Thought for the day: When we think we have nothing, we have hope in Christ; and hope is everything.

Link2Life: *Spend time visiting housebound members of your church.*
Elena Kalashnikova (Pskov, Russia)

A Father Who Cares

Read Ephesians 3:14–21
Cast all your anxiety on him because he cares for you.
1 Peter 5:7 (NIV)

On Sunday, the pastor spoke about the importance of being an honourable and trustworthy father. Tears slid down my face, but I brushed them away. Although I felt the pain of an unfulfilled relationship, I was hesitant to acknowledge my hurt.

As a child, I had learned that my father didn't want me. I needed him, but he could do without me. His lack of affection made the concept of love difficult to understand. Over time, I became obsessed as I searched for someone to fill the void.

'Why did I come to church today?' I said under my breath. 'What am I doing here?' I wish someone would love me and take away my pain. I need a father.

Then I sensed the Holy Spirit whispering, 'You have a father. God is your father. He will make everything right for you.'

A calm, peaceful feeling settled over my spirit when I heard those words. Now, when I'm overwhelmed by the issues of life and need someone to lean on, I can rest in the arms of my heavenly Father. God is the father I have always wanted and needed.

Prayer: *Thank you, God, for loving us through the pain of loss. Amen*

Thought for the day: God is never too far away to comfort us.

Phoebe Leggett (South Carolina, US)

Honest Prayer

Read Psalm 4:1–8

Hannah replied, 'I'm just a very sad woman. I… have been pouring out my heart to the Lord.'
1 Samuel 1:15 (CEB)

Psalm 4 begins with an anguished cry and ends with joy and peace, found in the safety of God's arms. Often our prayers have the same pattern. We cry out to God and pour out our deepest feelings, turning them over to him.

Were you brought up to let it all out before God? I wasn't. No self-respecting farm boy would express emotions to anyone, certainly not to God. Sometimes, I didn't even know I had feelings.

My wife, Jan, helped me to learn. Soon after we met, she asked how I felt. I had no idea. Over time, I watched her pour out her feelings to God and to me. I discovered that once she did, she could let them go. Then I tried expressing my feelings to God. What a wonderful revelation!

When I read the psalms in earnest, I see honest prayer in nearly every verse. I see utter honesty in Jesus' prayer from the cross: 'My God, my God, why have you forsaken me?' (Psalm 22:1, NRSV). Even on the cross, in his dying breaths, Jesus showed us the way to the father with deep, honest prayer. I'm sure God didn't flinch at Jesus' cry. It only tightened his loving embrace. So it is with us.

Prayer: *Dear God, open us up to say how we feel. Amen*

Thought for the day: The psalms can teach us to pray honestly.

Dan G. Johnson (Florida, US)

I Belong

Read Romans 8:11–17
You are no longer strangers and aliens... you are fellow citizens with God's people, and you belong to God's household.
Ephesians 2:19 (CEB)

My first memory of being different centres on a scar on my right wrist. All through my early years, I was positive that the only thing people saw when they looked at me was an ugly line flanked by polka dots where stitches once had been knotted. I was sure that my scar, my flaw, flashed as brightly as a neon sign.

However, as I grew and matured, I began identifying with other 'marks'—a mark of baptism on my forehead; a mark of confirmation on my heart; a mark of discipleship within my spirit. Gradually, I stopped thinking about that scar that had held me in its little shackled grip for far too long.

The scar on my wrist has faded somewhat. The fear of not belonging that it once represented has faded as well. It has been replaced by a new sense of belonging—related to the Spirit and belonging to the family of God. As part of a group of Christian believers who practise acceptance and love, I need not fear being odd. In this family, we discover each other's scratches and gashes—some visible on the outside, some hidden in the heart. No matter which, God's radiant, life-giving, life-bearing Spirit working among believers turns those scars into marks that stand for healing.

Prayer: *Dear God, help us to see ourselves the way you see us—as your beloved children, flaws and all. Amen*

Thought for the day: We are all beloved children of God.

Link2Life: *Pinpoint a time you identified yourself as different. Was the difference based on fear or love?*

Julia A. Halstead (Tennessee, US)

Footprints of Faith

Read Hebrews 12:1–2

Jesus said, 'I am the way, and the truth, and the life. No one comes to the Father except through me.'
John 14:6 (NRSV)

For a long time our province has suffered from the volcanic ash spewing from the Puyehue volcano. We can see the ash particularly on the dark-hued rooftops and other dark surfaces, including the ramp leading to the entrance of our church. One day as I stepped onto the ramp, I saw footprints made by the people who had arrived earlier. That observation led me to remember those who had preceded me on this great journey of faith. In addition to their faithful witness, they left tangible 'footprints', such as the construction of churches and schools, the forming of church choirs and many other works of faith that have contributed to our life of Christian discipleship.

I am grateful to the pioneers of the faith who led the way for my spiritual formation. Just as they faithfully walked the path God set before them, I too must continue my journey and leave footprints of faith.

Prayer: *Dear Lord, help us recognise the footprints of the faithful who came before us so that we may follow their example. Amen*

Thought for the day: The footprints of others can guide us in our walk of faith.

Luis Alberto Jones (Chubut, Argentina)

The Work

Read John 17:1–5

I have brought you glory on earth by finishing the work you gave me to do.
John 17:4 (NIV)

Visiting Africa on a recent mission trip was an incredible experience, while at the same time very disheartening. Starvation, sickness and general poverty abound; and the needs of the people are overwhelming. Our team offered aid in various ways, but I despaired of making a difference.

One morning, while preparing to work in a very poor village, I read John 17:1–5. As I read Jesus' prayer about the work he had been given to do, I was flooded with a sense of his love for the Father and his love for the world. Jesus embraced the work he was given to do on earth, leaving its outcome in his Father's hands—an outcome that turned out to be more wonderful than any of us could have imagined.

The work God has given each of us to do will be difficult at times. But we can share Jesus Christ's goal—to bring God glory on earth. God can and will make all the difference. To work with all our might 'as though you were serving the Lord' (Ephesians 6:7, CEB) is the way to glorify the Father. The outcome is completely in God's hands, and it will be more wonderful than any of us can imagine.

Prayer: *Dear God, giver of all good gifts, help us to embrace the work you have given us to do. In Jesus' name. Amen*

Thought for the day: We glorify God by our obedience.

Karin Hust (California, US)

Spiritual Sowing and Growing

Read Matthew 13:3–9

[Some] seeds fell on good soil and brought forth grain, some a hundred-fold, some sixty, some thirty.
Matthew 13:8 (NRSV)

After moving to a new house, we started cleaning the land behind the house for cultivation. We removed grass, shrubs and stones. However, within two weeks of cleaning, new grass began to appear. Cutting the grass was not enough; we needed to remove the grass by pulling out the roots to make sure it would not grow again. I removed as much of the grass as I could. The grass appeared again but this time more sparsely. After several cleanings, the land became good ground for sowing new seeds.

I began thinking about this incident in a spiritual context. In order to bear fruit, my heart needs to be receptive to spiritual seed. I need to pull up the weeds of worldly passions. Addressing these issues superficially is not enough; they need to be addressed at their roots. As these desires gradually change, I am better able to receive new spiritual seeds. This transformation is a slow process that takes time. Even so, I am encouraged to see the worldliness slowly losing its hold on me and the spiritual seeds taking root.

Prayer: *Dear God, prepare our hearts to receive the spiritual seed of your word. In Jesus' name we pray. Amen*

Thought for the day: Spiritual transformation takes time and patience.

Pramila Barkataki (Uttar Pradesh, India)

PRAYER FOCUS: THOSE SEEKING SPIRITUAL TRANSFORMATION

Eternal Hope

Read John 14:15–19

Jesus said, 'Because I live, you also will live.'
John 14:19 (NIV)

In the time since my mother died, I have thought of her and missed our times together. Thankfully, I am surrounded by many things that offer comfort: the colourful patchwork quilt, pieced together by her hands, that brightens my bed; the rose bush that started as a cutting from her garden; the loving note she placed in a safe-deposit box for me that read, 'Trusting in God and walking by faith can carry you far. A mother's love never dies.' Certainly the greatest comfort of all is the promise of Jesus Christ that gave her hope for so many years: 'Because I live, you also will live.'

I know that I will continue to miss my mother. It is natural to feel the loss of those we love so much, but through faith in God we can experience joy even in times of sorrow.

Prayer: *O God, you comfort us in our grief and lift us up in our despair. Thank you for the great hope we find in our risen Saviour as we pray, 'Our Father which art in heaven, Hallowed be thy name. Thy kingdom come. Thy will be done in earth, as it is in heaven. Give us this day our daily bread. And forgive us our debts, as we forgive our debtors. And lead us not into temptation, but deliver us from evil: For thine is the kingdom, and the power, and the glory, for ever.'* * *Amen*

Thought for the day: Christ's victory over death gives us hope in any sorrow.

Barry N. Hopkins (Georgia, US)

PRAYER FOCUS: SOMEONE WHOSE PARENT HAS DIED
* Matthew 6:9–13 (KJV)

Broken for Me

Read Psalm 51:1–12

The sacrifice acceptable to God is a broken spirit; a broken and contrite heart, O God, you will not despise.
Psalm 51:17 (NRSV)

Offering me the bread at Holy Communion, the server declared, 'The body of Christ, broken for you.'

Deep within my spirit, a voice responded, 'It's OK to be broken, Sandy.' Those words at the Communion table connected me unmistakably to Jesus Christ and the cross.

I experience brokenness each time my selfish, sinful nature asserts itself, and I ignore God's instruction. Then, other voices—anxiety, self-condemnation or anger—join the conversation within me, while I struggle to restore confidence in myself with rationalisation and reason. The outcome of this drama is that I am a defeated, broken Christian.

But God hears my internal conversations, and has provided a cure for my brokenness. Because of Jesus' sacrifice, I can stand in the presence of God knowing that I am neither rejected nor condemned. As I confess my sin, repenting in faith like David in Psalm 51, God replaces my guilt and brokenness with the righteousness of Christ. I am restored, and I feel truly loved once more by my Creator.

Prayer: *O God, thank you that the broken bread of Communion reminds me of my brokenness and my need to repent. Forgive me for my sin, Lord. Amen*

Thought for the day: In Christ our brokenness is made whole.

Sandra Bartz (Ohio, US)

That's Theology!

Read 1 Corinthians 1:18–25

The Lord says... Therefore once more I will astound these people with wonder upon wonder; the wisdom of the wise will perish, the intelligence of the intelligent will vanish.

Isaiah 29:14 (NIV)

For much of my life I paid little attention to theology. I read the Bible and books about the Bible, but theology seemed academic, uninteresting. Then a few years ago, worried that I had missed something, I began to read about theology and famous theologians. I learned how Irenaeus of Lyons and Augustine of Hippo influenced early Christian doctrine. I read about Luther, Calvin and Zwingli and the profound effects their ideas had on Christian thought. I read the ideas of more modern theologians such as F.D.E. Schleiermacher, Paul Tillich and Karl Barth, and I even understood some of what they wrote.

Yes, I discovered I had been missing the deepening experience of disciplined inquiry into God's interaction with us. I learned that when faithful people, inspired by the Holy Spirit, think about God, a light begins to shine in the darkness (see John 1:5).

Theologians regularly quarrel. But who's right? Theology itself moves into and out of varying patterns of belief. It illuminates the path so well that a seeker of truth easily forgets the destination. Christians in Corinth had fallen into this trap. They came from widely varying backgrounds and faced many rival claims to Christian wisdom. So Paul resorted to the basics. 'We preach Christ crucified,' he told the Corinthians. That's truth. That's theology!

Prayer: *Gracious Lord, help us remember that wisdom begins at the cross of Jesus and remains eternally there. Amen*

Thought for the day: What expands my faith and deepens my understanding?

Bob Tippee (Texas, US)

Picture Perfect

Read Psalm 139:13–18

Your eyes beheld my unformed substance. In your book were written all the days that were formed for me, when none of them as yet existed.
Psalm 139:16 (NRSV)

My two-year-old daughter loves me to read to her. She stands, hands outstretched, in front of the cupboard where we keep her books, and yells, 'Book, book, book!' I pick her up to let her choose the book she wants. Then she snuggles into my lap, and we read together.

One of her favourite books is her photo album. She loves looking at pictures of herself as a baby or seeing pictures of herself in her prettiest dress, with her granddad, or in her daddy's arms. My daughter has seen pictures from the ultrasound I had before she was born. As we look through the photos, I tell her what was happening when the pictures were taken.

The Bible says that God has a book about us, in which all the days of our life were written down before we were born. I imagine that God's book is a little like my daughter's photo album, filled with the places he wants me to see and the people he wants me to help. I look forward to seeing, one day in heaven, what is written about me in God's book. I hope to read that I lived up to the good plans he had for me on earth.

Prayer: *Thank you, God, for designing our bodies and our lives. Help us to live up to your plans and purposes for us. Amen*

Thought for the day: God has a purpose for my life.

Emma Angela Athyala (Auckland, New Zealand)

Never Left Out

Read Matthew 28:1–8

The angel said to the women… 'Go quickly and tell his disciples: "He has risen from the dead and is going ahead of you into Galilee. There you will see him." '
Matthew 28:7 (NIV)

An angel first proclaimed the good news to the women at the tomb, but none of the twelve disciples who left everything to follow Jesus were there. They were told only later that they had to wait to see this good news for themselves and that they would need to travel to another region to do so. I wondered why Jesus' closest followers were left out of the story.

I know what it feels like to be left out. For nearly ten years my wife and I longed to be parents. Finally, we had an opportunity to foster children who came into the care of child protective services, with a view to adopting them. Four children have come into our home, but each one has returned to their respective biological families. We cannot help but ask ourselves sometimes, 'Why are we being left out?'

The truth is—we're not. Just because the disciples did not see Jesus straight away, it didn't mean that he hadn't risen, hadn't defeated death itself and hadn't brought hope for new life to everyone. It meant only that Jesus was waiting for the right time to reveal himself in another unique and special way.

The disciples were not left out; my wife and I are not left out. It may seem as if God is doing something miraculous for everyone but us—but take heart! Even before we see God, we can already receive his life-giving power.

Prayer: *Mighty God, remind us of your power even when we do not see it. Amen*

Thought for the day: We are always in God's care.

Tim A. Gould (Texas, US)

A Father's Love

Read 1 John 4:7–12
The only thing that counts is faith expressing itself through love.
Galatians 5:6 (NIV)

I was waiting outside the hospital ward as the nurse tended my 92-year-old father. 'Who's that pretty young lady out there?' the nurse asked about me, though I am neither pretty nor young. To my surprise, my father replied, 'A very dear friend.' I realised then that dementia was taking its toll; he was beginning to forget who I am. But in spite of the dementia, he never forgot to say, 'I love you.'

When his prostate cancer turned aggressive, I knew he didn't have much longer to live. Just hours before he died, he suddenly mouthed the words, 'I love you, Marilyn.' He was too weak to say the words out loud, but I could read his lips easily.

Caring for a loved one with dementia is difficult. But the love of God gives us moments of grace that shine a little light into the darkness. Like a loving parent, God cares for us unfailingly throughout our lives. 'If we love one another,' says the apostle John, 'God lives in us and his love is made complete in us' (1 John 4:12).

Prayer: *Help us, Lord, to show your love in the difficult relationships in our lives. Amen*

Thought for the day: Who needs to hear you say, 'I love you'?

Link2Life: *Spend time with an elderly person to allow his or her carer a time of respite.*

Marilyn McGinnis (California, US)

Tell Them God Loves Them

Read 2 Corinthians 5:16–21

In Christ God was reconciling the world to himself, not counting their trespasses against them, and entrusting the message of reconciliation to us.

2 Corinthians 5:19 (NRSV)

During the 1980s, a group of prominent nationalist Afrikaners met with Bishop Desmond Tutu. The meeting was to introduce young Afrikaner leaders to what was then called 'the struggle'. The participants heard the life stories and viewpoints of their compatriots, and stayed with people from the townships. They saw the devastating effects of apartheid on the lives of ordinary black people. They also discovered (and for many this left the deepest impression) that despite the Afrikaners' role in maintaining apartheid, the black people they met did not bear personal animosity toward them. On the contrary, they welcomed them with generosity and forgiveness.

Bishop Tutu told them, 'Please go and tell your people that God loves them, that they are extremely valuable and important in God's eyes, and that they should never forget this… If they can discover and embrace this, they will also have the faith and courage to view all other people in the same way.'

Not only did the message leave a lasting impression, it changed lives, helping people to see their God-given worth and to appreciate it in others. The participants gained a new perspective on those they had viewed as dangerous enemies and labelled 'communists' and 'terrorists'.

Prayer: *Dear God, teach us to love one another as you love us, in the name of Jesus Christ. Amen*

Thought for the day: Look beyond labels to love the people who bear them.

Carel Anthonissen (Western Cape, South Africa)

The End is Near!

Read 1 Peter 4:7–11
The end of all things is near.
1 Peter 4:7 (NIV)

Every once in a while someone announces publicly that the world will end soon. A few preachers even predict an exact date. People respond to such predictions in various ways: most disregard them; others mock them; some hoard survival supplies or give away their possessions as they await the end.

In today's reading, written 20 centuries ago, Peter tells us, 'The end of all things is near.' From his point of view, we are never far from the fulfilment of all things in Jesus Christ—the end is always near. So as I considered this passage, I was eager to discover how Peter advises us to live here and now. What is the best way today to prepare for the end of the world?

Rather than urging us to stockpile food or dispose of property, Peter encourages us to pray with a clear mind; to love others deeply; to serve wholeheartedly with our God-given abilities. The best preparation for the end of the world is to keep praying, loving and serving so that 'in all things God may be praised through Jesus Christ' (1 Peter 4:11).

Prayer: *With joy we anticipate the fulfilment of your return, Lord Jesus. As we watch for you, we give ourselves to alert prayer and loving service. Amen*

Thought for the day: The end is near—therefore pray, love, serve.

Marion Speicher Brown (Florida, US)

Learning to Trust

Read 1 John 4:9–19

We love because [God] first loved us.

1 John 4:19 (NRSV)

For many years I have kept part of a friend's letter in which she described how she had lovingly cared for a timid, stray cat. At first it was extremely fearful and suspicious and kept its distance from her. But gradually the cat became less afraid and even allowed my friend to handle her kittens from the very first day they were born. The cat had learned to trust my friend completely because of the constant love my friend gave her.

We can see in this a picture of God reaching out to us with constant love. How do we respond—by backing away from him, keeping our distance, always afraid? Or do we respond by gradually drawing nearer and nearer because we have learned to trust him? When we receive the love God offers us through our Lord Jesus Christ and learn to trust completely, he teaches us to love one another so that people around us may also experience this love. 'If we love one another, God lives in us, and his love is perfected in us' (1 John 4:12).

It is a wonderful transformation when love drives out fear (see 1 John 4:18) and replaces it with trust.

Prayer: *Thank you, Christ Jesus, that you have come to be our friend as well as our Saviour, loving us so completely that we can trust you with all that is dearest to us. Amen*

Thought for the day: God's love can drive away our fears.

Hazel V. Thompson (Somerset, England)

Peace at Last

Read Psalm 37:1–11

Let the peace of Christ rule in your hearts, to which indeed you were called in the one body. And be thankful.
Colossians 3:15 (NRSV)

I have never been patient. Even in childhood, I met any situation I didn't like with quick anger; this only grew worse as I aged. I lost jobs, friends and girlfriends because of my anger. When a health condition forced me to stop working, my anger increased. I felt trapped, frustrated with myself and helpless, yet I did not know how to change.

Then one day I met a young pastor who, unlike almost everyone else I knew, did not flinch and leave when I became angry. Instead he told me gently, 'I can help you cool the anger that is burning you alive.' Amazed and intrigued, I was willing to listen to this calm voice.

He took me to a Bible study group at his church. The people accepted me and truly cared about me. As I studied scripture regularly I began to feel at peace for the first time. This was the life I wanted, and from that day on, I have been able to better control my anger, though it is an ongoing process. I have not looked back. After years of anger, I finally found peace through studying the words of scripture with a group of people who love me as I am.

Prayer: *Dear God, always let the words of your love be stronger than our hatred. Amen*

Thought for the day: God's peace is priceless.

Mark A. Carter (Texas, US)

The Sparrows are Back

Read Matthew 6:25–34
God is our refuge and strength, an ever-present help in trouble.
Psalm 46:1 (NIV)

Years ago, we had flocks of sparrows in the garden. They bathed in the birdbath and dried off on the fence. At other times they'd take dust baths in our Japanese-style garden. This year, again, we have had ten or more sparrows in at a time, plus three batches of babies who constantly chirp for mum or dad to feed them. Perhaps news has got out that our garden is a safe place with plenty of food and water.

The news is out for Christians as well. We have a refuge where we can rest without fear or worry. If God can take care of the sparrows and count the hairs on our heads, then he is able to take care of us.

The sparrows that visit our home fill the air with their songs and have no worry about meeting their needs or sowing or reaping their food. They greet the dawn with notes of joy. If God takes care of the birds, how much more will we be taken care of? When we worry, we lose our joy and effectiveness. When instead we have faith in God to meet our needs and put him first in our lives, then we can focus our energy on glorifying our Creator.

Prayer: *Sustainer of all, you are the one who feeds the birds and dresses the flowers, so we know you will take care of us. Amen*

Thought for the day: In God we have a safe place.

V. Louise Cunningham (Washington, US)

True Riches

Read Luke 19:1–10

Give, and it will be given to you. A good measure, pressed down, shaken together, running over, will be put into your lap; for the measure you give will be the measure you get back.
Luke 6:38 (NRSV)

A little boy outside the supermarket was clutching some sports cards that the shop was giving out as a promotion. He wanted to give an extra one to another child. His mother objected. 'Giving doesn't make you rich,' she said. This bit of folk wisdom had convinced her but not her son. She then took her son—and the cards—and walked forcefully away. Neither she nor the boy looked happy.

What a contrast this scene was to Zacchaeus' experience! Zacchaeus discovered that giving did make him rich, indeed. He prepared a meal for Jesus and his followers. He promised Jesus that he would give half of his possessions to the poor. Zacchaeus gave from a heart overflowing with joy and gratitude for the new life Jesus had given him.

If they had had sports cards in ancient Jericho, no doubt Zacchaeus would have given away his extra one—and walked away happy!

Prayer: *Wondrous God, teach us to give freely, as you do. In Jesus' name. Amen*

Thought for the day: Sharing God's love with others makes us rich.

Mary van Rheenen (Gelderland, The Netherlands)

Trustworthy God

Read Psalm 31:1–5

Into your hands I commit my spirit; deliver me, Lord, my faithful God.
Psalm 31:5 (NIV)

I stepped onto the diving board and stood at the edge for several minutes as I prepared to take my first dive into the college pool. Trying to relax and remember the techniques from my swimming classes, I still felt nervous.

'Don't be afraid,' my swimming coach yelled as he waited for me to dive. 'Remember, I'm right here to help you.' When I heard my coach's words, I decided to dive in, feeling confident that he would assist me if I encountered any problems.

As I recalled this situation, I thought about Jesus as he prayed in the garden of Gethsemane. Feeling afraid, he prayed, 'Take this cup from me.' But he also must have known that he could trust his heavenly Father completely and that his Father would deliver him, even in death, because he continued, 'Yet not what I will, but what you will' (Mark 14:36).

As we journey through life, we will encounter troubles and danger. But just as Jesus trusted God in his darkest hour, we, too, can remain confident in God's promise to take care of us during this life and the life to come.

Prayer: *Dear steadfast and loving God, may we learn to trust you in every circumstance. Amen*

Thought for the day: Even when others forsake us, we can still trust God.

James C. Hendrix (Indiana, US)

The Light in Life

Read John 1:1–5

Jesus [said], 'I am the light of the world. Whoever follows me will never walk in darkness but will have the light of life.'
John 8:12 (NRSV)

I have been in prison for more than eight years, but for me the day of reckoning came when my marriage ended in divorce five years ago. That meant I had lost my son for ever. This drove me into an abyss of despair. Thoughts of suicide lingered in my mind continually. I lived in both physical and emotional darkness.

After trying to pray, that night I dreamed that an unidentified light healed the wounds of my heart. Today I know that light was Jesus Christ. From the time of that experience to today, I faithfully pray. Also, I joined an English Bible study that meets twice a week. Gradually the wounds in my heart have begun to heal, as I have come to understand what it means for God to accompany us when we are walking through our darkest times (see Psalm 23:4).

What a surprise I had this year before we celebrated the Chinese New Year! My ex-wife and my son whom I had not seen for five years came to pay me a visit. How does one describe this amazing grace? Now I am even more deeply convinced that Christ is the light that guides me and will give me a brighter future. Christ is the light of my life!

Prayer: *O Lord, thank you for lighting our path. We can walk into the future because you are our light. Amen*

Thought for the day: Christ shines light into our darkness.

Rake Hseuh (Hualien, Taiwan)

The Little Things

Read Hebrews 4:14–16

Are not all angels ministering spirits sent to serve those who will inherit salvation?

Hebrews 1:14 (NIV)

I was returning from a trip abroad and on my way home I had to take a coach from Heathrow to Wolverhampton, and then a train journey. I was struggling with my large suitcase because, although it had wheels, the pull-up handle was well and truly stuck. During the bus journey I worried as to how I would manage to walk the distance from the bus terminal to the railway station. I prayed: 'Please, Lord, send an angel to help me with my suitcase.'

When I got off the bus the driver lifted my case for me and I tried in vain to pull up the handle. Then I started to walk, struggling and dragging. A young woman passing stopped, took over my case and walked with me to the railway station, where my train was just coming in. I said to my helper, 'Thank you. You are an angel!' She just smiled as I got on the train, and when I turned round to say goodbye she had completely disappeared.

While we had been walking she had not attempted to make conversation, and she had nothing with her, not even a handbag. I felt humbled and thanked God that he cares so much for us and the little things of our lives.

Prayer: *Thank you, Lord Jesus, that you care about each one of your children and our daily needs. Help me to be unselfish and caring toward others. Amen*

Thought for the day: I will thank God for all his care toward me today and every day.

Pat Rantisi (Shropshire, England)

From Darkness to Light

Read John 1:1–18

I have come into the world as a light, so that everyone who believes in me should not stay in darkness.
John 12:46 (NRSV)

I was four years old at the time, but it is still one of my most vivid memories. My family was visiting the pilgrimage site of Rachel's tomb in the West Bank during Holy Week along with hundreds of other people (see Genesis 35:19–20). Darkness closed in around me as the crush of people surged toward the tomb. As we approached the tomb the surging mass of humanity tried to pull me away, but the strong grip of my mother's hand kept us together. I cried for help, and my father managed to reach me and lift me above the darkness to where I could see the light. Dad carried me on his back until we were free from the crowds and it was safe to let me walk on my own.

Our Christian faith teaches us to have hope even in times of darkness. When Jesus was crucified, it seemed as though darkness had won. But the tomb was not the end. With Jesus' resurrection light overcame the darkness. Sometimes it seems that the darkness has overcome us, but when we call out, God can lift us up above the darkness so that we can experience the light.

Prayer: *Dear eternal God, we thank you that no matter how the darkness seems to surround us, you are always there to lead us into the light. We pray as Jesus taught us, saying, 'Our Father in heaven, hallowed be your name, your kingdom come, your will be done on earth as it is in heaven. Give us today our daily bread. Forgive us our debts, as we also have forgiven our debtors. And lead us not into temptation, but deliver us from the evil one.'* Amen*

Thought for the day: God never abandons us to the darkness.

Gordon Paul Page (Illinois, US)

PRAYER FOCUS: VISITORS TO THE HOLY LAND

* Matthew 6:9–13 (NIV)

Hope's Reward

Read 1 Peter 1:3–7

Hope does not disappoint us, because God's love has been poured into our hearts through the Holy Spirit that has been given to us.
Romans 5:5 (NRSV)

As an avid amateur gardener, I was excited to take on the large garden around our new home. Rainfall was sparse and for almost five years I struggled to grow vegetables and flowers in the hot, arid climate and extremely poor soil. I often felt as if I were fighting a losing battle: what the scorching heat did not cause to dry up and die, the roaming livestock chewed and trampled into the dirt. Eventually, I was forced to give up my dream of a lush garden outdoors and to settle for potted plants inside the house and on the front porch.

One day I looked wistfully out of the kitchen window at the brown grass stubble where my garden should have been. To my amazement, I saw in the middle of it a single, brilliant red flower coming from a leafless stalk. A hibiscus shrub I had long ago stopped watering and thought was dead had somehow put out a solitary blossom. What a beautiful and encouraging sight! What a symbol of hope!

In the years since, I've often thought about that hibiscus shrub and compared it to some of life's situations that we tend to give up on: a broken marriage, a rebellious child, a dead-end job. Yet God's word gives us assurance that even in these seemingly hopeless circumstances we can have hope that someday, one day, our situation—like my lone hibiscus flower—will start blooming again.

Prayer: *O God, help us to continue to put our trust in you and the hope you have given us in Jesus Christ. Amen*

Thought for the day: When we are beyond hope, God is waiting to encourage us.

Arlene Henry (British West Indies)

Attitude

Read Matthew 6:9–15

Be kind to one another, tender-hearted, forgiving one another, as God in Christ has forgiven you.
Ephesians 4:32 (NRSV)

Each Sunday during worship we respond to the minister and to one another by saying, 'In the name of Jesus Christ, you are forgiven.' This is the core of the service as well as the message. Paul made it clear that forgiving one another is important. But I've struggled with forgiving.

I hated the Americans who massacred so many people, including my sister, with the atomic bomb when I was 14. For many years I could neither forgive nor forget what they had done. But as I started to read the Bible, I was challenged and changed by the words of Jesus, 'Father forgive them, for they don't know what they're doing' (Luke 23:34, CEB).

In the Lord's Prayer we pray for God's kingdom to come and for his will to be done. We ask for our daily food, forgiveness and salvation from evil. Then we affirm God's dominion, power and glory. For me, forgiveness is a strong and powerful attitude.

Paul said, 'Be kind to one another' and 'tender-hearted'. When we allow God to make our hearts tender, we become able to forgive. For me forgiveness is given so strongly and so powerfully from God through Jesus that it breaks through the hatred caused by the atomic bomb.

Prayer: *Dear God, help us to understand how our attitudes and choices affect what happens in the world around us. Amen*

Thought for the day: God gives us the ability to make peace and to make war. Which will we choose?

Haruyoshi Fujimoto (California, US)

Pass it On

Read Isaiah 49:8–13

Sing for joy, O heavens, and exult, O earth; break forth, O mountains, into singing! For the Lord has comforted his people, and will have compassion on his suffering ones.

Isaiah 49:13 (NRSV)

Stuck in the pages of my Bible are many meditations from *The Upper Room*. Words written by people around the world have inspired me as I read them again and sometimes share them with a friend. Today I am looking at a prayer workshop article from 2007 entitled, 'Our Children, God's Children'. I have re-read this article over the years as we have experienced conflict in our family. Mental illness, estrangement and one son's loss of faith have torn us apart. Today I think of my friend, Pat, who is living through great pain with her children and grandchildren. I decide to take her to lunch and give her the article, praying that the words will lift her as they have often lifted me.

In 2 Corinthians 1:4, Paul describes God as one 'who consoles us in all our affliction, so that we may be able to console those who are in any affliction with the consolation with which we ourselves are consoled by God'. God wants to comfort us so that we are then able to pass on his comfort to another. Our wonderful God works through imperfect people like you and me. Even in our brokenness we can serve him. Even our pain can be a gift when we receive God's comfort and pass it on to another.

Prayer: *Dear Lord, lead us today to someone who needs your strengthening word. Amen*

Thought for the day: Who needs to receive God's comfort through me today?

Eleanor Cowles (Oregon, US)

We are All Needed

Read 1 Corinthians 12:14–26a

If one part suffers, every part suffers with it.
1 Corinthians 12:26a (NIV)

I fell and broke my hip recently, so I was fairly immobile for a while and fully reliant on other people while the healing took place. During that time I realised the truth of Paul's words about the body: 'If one part suffers, every part suffers with it.' Indeed they do; as I used various pieces of medical equipment to help me move, my good leg, arms, shoulders and wrists had to work a lot harder. In fact, they ached more than the damaged leg.

Paul compared the body to the Church. While I was out of action, other people in our fellowship took on things that I would normally have done. We are all needed to play our part in the church family, and in our own families, as my husband and children discovered.

As I remembered all the love and support expressed to me at that time, more words of Paul came to my mind: 'From him the whole body, joined and held together by every supporting ligament, grows and builds itself up in love, as each part does its work' (Ephesians 4:16). I pray that when I am fully recovered, I will do my part to support others.

Prayer: *Dear Lord, thank you for blessing us with friends and family, and help us to be there for them when they need us. Amen*

Thought for the day: God works through all the times of our lives, through difficulties and through blessings.

Pamela Harrison (Conwy, North Wales)

How Do You Love God?

Read Mark 12:28–34

Be imitators of God, as beloved children, and live in love, as Christ loved us.

Ephesians 5:1–2 (NRSV)

I love to embrace our little son, to hold him tightly and to kiss him. Then I ask him, 'How do you love Daddy?' He puts his arms around my neck and cuddles up to me. My child loves me and demonstrates his love for me. This brings me enormous joy and happiness. When my son lies sleeping with his arms around my neck, I am prepared to sit still for a long time. The same feeling stirs in me when my son does what I ask of him.

How pleasant it is for our heavenly Father when we express our love and devotion to him with our whole heart, not only during our Sunday worship but also in our daily life, in each act and every thought. When we choose God's way rather than our way, he is pleased.

Prayer: *Dear Father, fill our hearts with more love for you. Help us express our love every day. Amen*

Thought for the day: Our expressions of obedient love please God.

Fedor Kim (Pskov, Russia)

Please Call

Read 1 Thessalonians 5:16–24
Pray continually.
1 Thessalonians 5:17 (NIV)

The phone sits silent. Why hasn't she called?

It had been several days since I had heard from my daughter. We had formed the habit of making contact, just to keep in touch. She leads a very busy life; so when I don't hear from her, I know she has simply forgotten. She would call if anything was wrong. But I miss her calls, however brief.

Suddenly it dawns on me. This is the way God must feel when I don't pray. Reminders of God's love surround me. But sometimes in the rush of everyday life I put off spending time in prayer or forget to thank him. God loves to hear from us. Whether in long prayers or short prayers, he wants to hear whatever is on our minds. He cares. He is interested and will help if he is asked. He is always there, waiting for my 'call'.

The telephone finally rang that day. When I heard my daughter's voice, my heart was filled with joy. I will never again think my prayers are too short, too long or too unimportant for God, who always receives them with love and joy.

Prayer: *Thank you, loving God, for always being ready to listen to us. Amen*

Thought for the day: God is with us even when we forget to pray.

Link2Life: *Call someone or send a card to a loved one.*

Sara Pursley (Texas, US)

A Complete Family

Read Galatians 3:23—4:7

For you did not receive a spirit of slavery to fall back into fear, but you have received a spirit of adoption.
Romans 8:15 (NRSV)

I always knew that I was an adopted child. My parents told me the story gradually, beginning when I was young. Finally, they told me about the day in the courtroom when the judge banged his gavel and announced that I was their child. I was lovingly adopted and joyfully incorporated into my family. I never had any reason to be concerned about my biological roots. Adoption was simply another way to be born into a family.

When I was older, I was amazed to discover that Paul described becoming a Christian as being adopted into God's family through Christ. If ever I had a conversion event in my faith, it was the sudden realisation that I was adopted into God's family, as truly as I was adopted into my earthly family.

When my two sons were at school, they asked if I knew anything about my biological parents. They wanted more information about their cultural roots and their health history. I researched their questions and provided them what little information I could find. But in the end, they decided that their adoption into God's family was most important.

Prayer: *Thank you, God, for being our loving parent and for keeping us, your children, close in all the situations of our lives; through Jesus Christ our Lord. Amen*

Thought for the day: Adoption into God's family provides us with courage and strength for living.

Barbara S. Cook (Kansas, US)

The Higher Power We Need

Read Luke 24:13–35

And he said to them, 'What are you discussing with each other while you walk along?' They stood still, looking sad.
Luke 24:17 (NRSV)

Divorce devastated me. I had grown up as the child of divorced parents and vowed that my children would never know that pain. Now my hope of building a happy family was destroyed.

But as I turned to God in my heartbreak, I was inspired to be the best single father I could be. Eventually my children came to live with me full time, and I was blessed to see them thriving and happy. Then I married a woman who shares my faith. Her love and wise partnership brought me healing. Together we have a healthy blended family.

The devastation I experienced at the end of my first marriage cannot compare to what the disciples must have felt when Jesus was executed. Not only was their teacher and friend gone, but so was their hope that he would restore their nation to powerful independence. But just as my sorrow was transformed into happiness, the disciples' grief and disappointment was replaced with joy when Jesus was raised to new life.

Christ is greater than our most debilitating sorrow. When our aspirations are crushed, he offers us the power of the resurrection, raising us up to renewed purpose, meaning and joy.

Prayer: *Help us, O Christ, to find in you the strength to overcome sorrow and the hope that will never disappoint. May we bear fruit that honours you. Amen*

Thought for the day: Christ calls us to new hope and life.

Clifford Rawley (Missouri, US)

PRAYER FOCUS: THOSE GOING THROUGH DIVORCE   113

Two Perspectives

Read Philippians 2:1–11

Let the same mind be in you that was in Christ Jesus.
Philippians 2:5 (NRSV)

We visited a museum while on holiday in Germany. I held my six-year-old daughter's hand as we walked up a staircase to the second floor. My eyes were fixed on the rather slippery marble steps when she looked up. 'Is that Jesus?' she asked.

I followed her stare and looked at a life-sized image of Christ on the cross, his head hanging down. In our church at home, the wooden cross was empty. My mind raced as I wondered how she had made the connection and also how I should answer. Her only comment in the meantime was very profound and very childlike: 'Such a poor, poor man!'

Immediately, I recalled my childhood parish church where there was a larger-than-life bronze image of Christ on the cross—head raised high, looking triumphantly into the distance.

Each image shows us a different perspective about the passage in Philippians 2. One perception is about a suffering man who is much like us when we are beaten down by this world. The second perception is about a man who through faith triumphs and is able to look beyond the present circumstances. Both are true. This is the Christ, the Saviour we follow into eternity.

Prayer: *Dear heavenly Father, grant us the grace and strength to keep looking beyond our present hardships towards the glorious future you are preparing for us. Let us be like Christ in our endurance. Amen*

Thought for the day: Christians look forward to an eternity with Christ.

Joanne Verhulst (Gelderland, The Netherlands)

God's Presence

Read Psalm 139:1–12

Where can I go from your spirit? Or where can I flee from your presence?
Psalm 139:7 (NRSV)

A few days ago I had a conversation with a friend about the tangible presence of God in our lives. My friend said that although he believed completely in God, Jesus and the Holy Spirit, he didn't really experience God in his daily life. After we parted, I couldn't get his words out of my mind.

'Do I sense God's presence with me each day?' I asked myself. I felt that I always could count on the Holy Spirit's comfort when I was stressed and asked for help. My spirit would always rejoice during the worship service in my church. And I always had a sense of God's presence when I was engaged in Christian service such as missions or teaching in Sunday school. But I had to admit that I did not really feel God's presence during my normal everyday routine.

Scripture teaches us that God is always with us. I also knew that the Holy Spirit guides us into all truth. I finally realised that guidance was available for me every second of every day, if I would just open my eyes and look for it. Now I experience God's presence every day by noticing opportunities to help others at every turn. I can do this at home and everywhere that my day-to-day activities take me.

Prayer: *Dear God, teach us to be aware of your presence with us at all times and in all our daily activities. Amen*

Thought for the day: Where can I see God's presence in my life today?

William E. Sears, III (Georgia, US)

Are We Listening?

Read 1 Samuel 3:1–10

David said further to his son Solomon, 'Be strong and of good courage, and act. Do not be afraid or dismayed; for the Lord God, my God, is with you.'
1 Chronicles 28:20 (NRSV)

In March 2011, I was going through a very difficult time. My mother had died of cancer after I had taken care of her for ten months. My relationship with my husband had deteriorated, and my spiritual life was at a low point. At that time, my out-of-control emotions made it difficult for me to hear the voice of God.

Especially in the midst of chaotic times, it is crucial that we take a moment from our daily schedule to listen to what God has to say. We can become so focused on our problems that we forget that God is always speaking to us—to our hearts, to our minds, to our spirits. It is even heartening to know this and to know that what God says is always for our good. We have but to be willing to listen.

I always try to be attentive to God's message filled with the assurances that I will receive help and that I am loved.

Prayer: *Compassionate God, bring calm to the chaotic state of our lives so that we can hear when you speak to us. Amen*

Thought for the day: God is always speaking to us.

Elba I. González (Puerto Rico)

Reason for Rejoicing

Read James 1:2–5

Consider it pure joy, my brothers and sisters, whenever you face trials of many kinds, because you know that the testing of your faith produces perseverance.
James 1:2–3 (NIV)

It was a productive morning. However, shortly before lunch, I interrupted my sermon preparation to check on something with my wife. I went downstairs and discovered her cleaning up water that had flooded the basement floor.

I had recently repaired the washing machine, so I knew my lack of thoroughness had probably caused the problem. My reaction was anger—at myself for my carelessness, and at the situation because cleaning up the water would waste valuable time.

My anger didn't change anything. I wasted energy and emotion that could have gone toward our cleaning efforts. And my anger no doubt affected my sermon preparations.

When we are disappointed, frustrated or have unexpected trials, it's easy to become needlessly angry. However, if we obey the word of God and rejoice even in our struggles, we'll have grace to endure the immediate trial. In addition, as we grow in endurance, the Lord will use it to make us 'mature and complete, not lacking anything' (James 1:4). That is reason for rejoicing.

Prayer: *When trials come to us, O God, help us not to focus on our anger but on your love and strength that not only help us to endure but to grow in our faith. Amen*

Thought for the day: God can use our struggles to strengthen our faith.

Robert C. Camenisch (Kentucky, US)

PRAYER FOCUS: THOSE WHOSE FAITH IS BEING TESTED

Culture Shock

Read Hebrews 11:1–3, 13–16

Jesus prayed, '[Those whom you gave me] are not of the world, even as I am not of it.'
John 17:16 (NRSV)

The language, food, social customs and national circumstances in 1966 Vietnam were strange to me. I was serving as a volunteer nurse in a small Christian hospital. Our patients were civilians suffering in the midst of the ongoing warfare in their country. We did what we could with the simple medical tools we had. Patients died of conditions easily treatable in my home country. I felt overwhelmed and depressed. Months later, I realised that I had been suffering from culture shock: feelings of rootlessness and instability that may result from sudden overwhelming change.

When I returned home to the US I discovered culture shock of a different type. I missed the quiet dignity and courage of the Vietnamese people—their respect for age and wisdom, their generosity and hospitality, the close ties of family and community, the simple and unshakeable faith in Jesus Christ that my Christian friends there had lived by.

As followers of Jesus Christ we will always live in culture shock. The writer of Hebrews reminds us that our faith in Christ makes us 'strangers and foreigners on the earth' (11:13). We will often—perhaps always—feel uncomfortable and out of place. For, we 'desire a better country… a heavenly one' (v. 16).

Prayer: *Dear God of all nations, disturb us from our earthly comfort. Help us to serve others with love even as we seek your heavenly home. Amen*

Thought for the day: Our discomfort with this world can lead us to help others in the name of Christ.

Mary Sue Rosenberger (Texas, US)

Are You Afraid to Die?

Read 1 Corinthians 15:51–55

Where, O death, is your victory? Where, O death, is your sting?
1 Corinthians 15:55 (NIV)

A few days before my father died of cancer, I went back to the Philippines to see him. His health was deteriorating and he was in unbearable pain, hardly able to utter words or to move. Nevertheless, he recognised me. As I watched him dying, I whispered, 'Dad, I love you. I hope you will trust in Christ alone.' He replied in a weak and slow whisper, 'I always do. I love you, son.' Three days later, he died peacefully.

We often don't want to face the realities of death. Because of his love for us, Jesus endured the agony and pain of crucifixion. Ultimately, Jesus entrusted his spirit to God. Three days later, he rose from the dead. If we trust our lives to Jesus Christ, we can have hope even as we face death. We have hope in Christ, who conquered death so that we will live eternally in his glory.

Prayer: *Dear Lord, help us to trust in you, fixing our eyes on the cross and hoping in the power of your resurrection. As Jesus taught us, we pray, 'Our Father which art in heaven, Hallowed be thy name. Thy kingdom come. Thy will be done, as in heaven, so in earth. Give us day by day our daily bread. And forgive us our sins; for we also forgive every one that is indebted to us. And lead us not into temptation; but deliver us from evil.'* Amen*

Thought for the day: 'Whether we live or die, we belong to the Lord' (Romans 14:8).

Brandon Manalo Vista (Auckland, New Zealand)

* Luke 11:2–4 (KJV)

God's Best

Read 2 Corinthians 12:7–10

The Lord said, 'My grace is sufficient for you, for power is made perfect in weakness.'
2 Corinthians 12:9 (NRSV)

My husband had high blood pressure and congestive heart failure, all complications of diabetes. He underwent a variety of tests, and the medical professionals sought a solution for each new complication. How reassuring to know that he was in the hospital, under the care of doctors who knew exactly what they were doing!

A sign posted in the hospital read, 'Our doctors are at their best when you are not.' This proved to be true when my husband became ill. Since reading the sign, I contemplate the thought that 'God is at his best when you are not'.

God knows what is happening in our lives when nothing makes sense to us, knows our weaknesses and understands our frustration and despair. In the Bible we can find what we need to see us through. The promises revealed in scripture offer us comfort and assurance. When you are having the most difficult experience possible, remember that 'God is at his best when you are not'.

Prayer: *God of power and healing, how reassuring to know you are with us! Grant that we never forget your goodness and power. In the name of Jesus, we pray. Amen*

Thought for the day: When we are not at our best, God is.

Maria Margarita Aguayo de Ortiz (Kentucky, US)

Possessions

Read Luke 12:22–34
Life does not consist in the abundance of possessions.
Luke 12:15 (NRSV)

The finance committee meeting had not gone well. The church did not have enough money, and we had to vote on what to cut. So we had some bitter discussions. I got home late at night, worn out, and was surprised to see my five-year-old son, David, still up. 'Dad, where have you been?'

I explained that we all earn money, save a little, spend a lot and give some to the Lord. And it seemed that people were not giving enough to the Lord, and the church was in some difficulty.

David did not seem to understand. But he was, after all, only five, so I went over it again: we earn money, save money, spend money and give some to the Lord. David still did not understand. Gently, I went over it again; but he still looked puzzled. Finally he said, 'Dad, I thought it was all the Lord's money!'

David's response completely changed the way I look at money and possessions. I started giving more and worrying less. Today none of my possessions means anything to me. All that matters are my family and friends, the church, and God—nothing else! This change in me has made my life easier and simpler.

Prayer: *Dear God of all creation, help us always to remember that all we have and all we are belong to you. Amen*

Thought for the day: Give more; worry less.

Link2Life: *Think of a charity to which you could offer some support.*

Chris Miller (Georgia, US)

A Blended Background

Read Exodus 2:1–10

'I have raised you up for this very purpose, that I might show you my power and that my name might be proclaimed in all the earth.'
Exodus 9:16 (NIV)

I'm an adopted Korean who grew up in the United States. My husband came to the US as an international student from Korea and remained there to work. Because of our backgrounds, we have been able to befriend other international families.

A year ago, we moved from California to South Korea for my husband's job. I was devastated to leave my former life. Now, we are living in South Korea, and I don't speak the language. I keep asking, 'Why am I here, God? What am I supposed to do?'

God reminded me of Moses, who was adopted by Pharaoh's daughter. Though a Hebrew, he was raised as an Egyptian. God used Moses and his blended culture in reaching out to and leading God's people.

'I have raised you up for this very purpose,' says Exodus 9:16. God has a purpose for me in Korea. I know part of it is to witness Christ's love to the people around me. As I pray and seek the Lord, God reveals little by little what I am to do. Whatever our circumstances and background, God has a plan and purpose for us.

Prayer: *Dear God, thank you for showing us that you can use us and our various cultural backgrounds. Help us to fulfil your purposes wherever we are. Amen*

Thought for the day: Each of us has a unique way to serve God.

Tina M. Cho (Seoul, South Korea)

Singing

Read Psalm 89:1–8

I will sing of the Lord's great love for ever; with my mouth I will make your faithfulness known through all generations.
Psalm 89:1 (NIV)

Recently my Bible readings for the day in two different books started with Psalm 89:1. The Bible reading at church also included the same verse. Three times in one day the Lord seemed to be saying to me that I should sing his praise for ever.

That was very encouraging, since I have always enjoyed singing. However, recently I have developed asthma and if I get a cold I need to take medication that has a nasty side effect: I lose my voice completely. I find this very frustrating because it becomes very difficult to sing praise to God when I have no voice.

Thinking and praying about the matter, I came to see that even if I have no voice physically to sing, I can still share my love of God through the written word, in poetry, by letters and by meditations such as this. I am still able to praise God and share his love with others.

Prayer: *Dear Lord, help me always to be ready to share your love either through the written, the spoken or the sung word. Amen*

Thought for the day: I will sing when I am able and still praise God when I cannot.

Link2Life: *Think of a practical way to share God's love with someone today.*

Hilary Hartley (Sussex, England)

Choosing Joy

Read Nehemiah 8:5–18

Do not be grieved, for the joy of the Lord is your strength.
Nehemiah 8:10 (NRSV)

I thought I was indispensible to my employer—until the day the company made me redundant. Morning walks, bike rides and getting involved in a women's Bible study group filled the first few months. However, sending out many job application forms and CVs brought no requests for interviews. I began to wonder who would hire a 63-year-old woman. Slowly, feelings of worthlessness began to depress me. Why was it so hard for me to enjoy doing things I wanted to?

While I was praying for encouragement, it was as if I heard God say, 'Do not grieve, for the joy of the Lord is your strength' (Nehemiah 8:10). Although Nehemiah faced considerable opposition during the rebuilding of Jerusalem's wall, he spent a lot of time on his knees, praying and trusting God. Nehemiah's example helped me to realise I could trust God for my income, a sense of personal worth and perhaps a new season in my life.

Choosing joy over giving in to despair meant finding delight in knowing God. This relationship gives me the strength to face my future. My grief changed to celebration of how abundantly God provides for me, so abundantly that I can share with others who need help too.

Prayer: *Work through me today, Lord Jesus, that I might be a blessing to someone. Amen*

Thought for the day: Choosing joy is worth the effort.

Sue Tornai (California, US)

Preparing a Room

Read John 14:1–4
'I go to prepare a place for you.'
John 14:2 (KJV)

My wife rushed me to the hospital when I suffered a heart attack. I do not remember anything from the time I left home until I regained consciousness. When I found myself in the hospital, with doctors, nurses and relatives around my bed, I realised that God had given me a new life.

I was quite comfortable in the hospital, but not as comfortable as I would be in my bed at home. When the doctors discharged me, my wife told me to stay while she went to prepare the bedroom for me. Then she would come back and take me home. She went ahead to prepare the room so that I would be comfortable.

My wife's preparing a room for me reminded me of Jesus' telling his disciples, 'I go to prepare a place for you.' When Jesus called his disciples, they left everything and followed him. How comforting it must have been for them when Jesus reassured them that they would one day have a room where they could rest with him!

I believe that in every situation, Jesus prepares a room for us. Sometimes, he moves ahead to prepare a room for us in a new situation to comfort us and to assure us of his presence.

Prayer: *Redeeming God, thank you for healing us, for giving us new life, and for making us comfortable in your home, through Jesus Christ. Amen*

Thought for the day: Jesus prepares a room for us.

Claudius Tewari (Uttar Pradesh, India)

Adversity or Opportunity?

Read 2 Corinthians 1:3–7

See, I have refined you, but not like silver; I have tested you in the furnace of adversity.

Isaiah 48:10 (NRSV)

In the last month, I have received too much sad news. My grandfather died, leaving behind my grandmother, to whom he had been married for over 70 years. My brother and his wife, parents of four children, are divorcing. My college-age daughters may not be coming home this summer. I have felt each successive loss press me farther down.

Then, in my Bible study group, someone called attention to a verse I had read but not considered: 'See, I have refined you, but not like silver; I have tested you in the furnace of adversity' (Isaiah 48:10). My adversity may not seem extreme to some. I have not lost a spouse to death or divorce. My daughters are taking a necessary step toward living as independent adults.

But not one of the events in my life is easy for me; my grief is real, if not extreme. Thinking about what God can help me to learn during this time has encouraged me. I have something to focus on besides the hurt. What might other people help me to see? Perhaps I can learn something about God's character and faithfulness as he walks with me through these days.

Prayer: *Thank you, God, for your word, which reminds us that you have our benefit in mind even in painful circumstances. Please help us to co-operate with you in the refining process and to be ready to comfort others as you have comforted us. Amen*

Thought for the day: I can look for opportunity in today's adversity.

Jennifer Aaron (Washington, US)

God's Grace

Read Ephesians 2:1–10

By grace you have been saved through faith, and this is not your own doing; it is the gift of God.
Ephesians 2:8 (NRSV)

Recently, I chose to travel on my birthday instead of having a party. A few months later, some friends arranged a day of surprises for me. We went to a musical, and the day ended with a fantastic party.

I was delighted, surprised and grateful; but I also felt that I didn't deserve all this. My friends had invested a great deal of planning and consideration in the celebration. My thought was, 'How will I ever be able to pay them back?'

My day of celebration reminds me of God's grace. My relationship with God is not about how well I am performing. Many times, I have felt that I am not good enough or that I don't deserve what he gives me. After all, God let his son Jesus Christ die on a cross for my sake.

I have learned to accept God's unconditional love, and to let him guide my life. When I can step back and let go, then I can feel that my life is meaningful and I can fully become a joy for others.

Prayer: *Dear God, you love us unconditionally. Help us to relax in your arms of grace and forgiveness. Amen*

Thought for the day: How can I convey God's unconditional love?

Annika Svensson (Kronoberg, Sweden)

A Glimpse of God

Read John 14:5–14

Jesus said, 'Anyone who has seen me has seen the Father.'
John 14:9 (NIV)

When my daughters joined the cast of a local Passion play, I volunteered as one of the supervisors for children in the cast. Throughout the production, I noticed the same reaction from viewers in every performance. When the actor who portrayed Jesus walked among the audience in one scene, people reached out to shake his hand. Some even held up their babies for him to touch as he walked by. And after the play was over, audience members sought him out.

The response to this young man illustrated the desire we have to see God—to know and be known by him. One day, we will see God face to face. Until that time, there are several ways to discover what our Creator is like. The Bible reveals God's nature, love, plans and goals for us. Prayer enables us to have a one-to-one relationship with him. The church provides opportunities for further instruction, encouragement, comfort and strength from other believers.

Most importantly, as we draw closer to Jesus, we get a glimpse of the Father, for Jesus is the 'radiance of God's glory and the exact representation of his being' (Hebrews 1:3).

Prayer: *Dear Jesus, you came to earth so that we could know the love of God and receive the gift of eternal life. Thank you for revealing God to us. Amen*

Thought for the day: God is always closer than we think.

Elaine T. Snider (Ohio, US)

God's Law Fulfilled

Read Romans 12:9–18

Serve one another humbly in love. For the entire law is fulfilled in keeping this one command: 'Love your neighbour as yourself.'
Galatians 5:13–14 (NIV)

I was excited to be going with my church mission team to work in a remote mountain village in Honduras. It could be reached only by horseback or on foot because the roadway had been washed away by a hurricane. Just as we rounded the last curve, I saw one of the most beautiful sights of my life. The entire village had turned out in their Sunday best to welcome us with wide smiles and a homemade banner that said, 'Bienvenido' (Welcome). As we dismounted, the children, shy at first, soon began to surround us as their parents shook our hands in greeting.

Our purpose was to build concrete floors to make life better in their homes. However, as we met and talked, I realised our true mission: to share God's love.

We accomplished the concrete work and hopefully improved life in 14 village homes. More importantly, while God helped us show love to those in need, I believe we received far more than we gave.

We can find purpose in life in many ways, but serving God's people in need is my chosen path. May we all look for opportunities to show God's love.

Prayer: *Dear God of compassion, thank you for every opportunity to show your love through serving others. Amen*

Thought for the day: When we give God's love to others, we receive it back a hundredfold.

Peter L. Banks (Georgia, US)

The Paper Cross

Read Mark 16:1–7

The message of the cross is foolishness to those who are perishing, but to us who are being saved it is the power of God.
1 Corinthians 1:18 (NIV)

Although she had spent three months in the hospital, my young daughter's health continued to decline because of an undiagnosed illness. I prayed daily as I sat beside her bed, watching her cry in pain.

One day, I went to the interfaith hospital chapel. As I knelt to pray, I felt a strong need to bow down before a cross, the symbol of power and faith and the assurance of Christ's presence with me. But there was no cross in the chapel. So I tore a piece of paper into the shape of a cross and set it before me as I knelt to pray for my daughter.

The cross represents the foundation of my Christian faith, the resurrected Jesus Christ. It reminds me that death has no victory and darkness has no sting; the cross guides me, empowers me, and equips me to face the valleys of my life. The cross, even a paper one marked with a mother's tears, is evidence, for me, of the love of God, the power of Jesus and the presence of the Holy Spirit.

Thanks be to God for his indescribable gift of love through Jesus Christ (see 2 Corinthians 9:15).

Prayer: *Lord of light, help us to remember the power of the cross when we feel helpless. Let the power of the cross live in us every day. Amen*

Thought for the day: Calvary is the starting point for all our journeys.

Malinda Fillingim (North Carolina, US)

Stormy Weather

Read Isaiah 43:1–5

You silence the roaring of the seas, the roaring of their waves, the tumult of the peoples.
Psalm 65:7 (NRSV)

When I was young, our three-week school holiday began in June—early winter in South Africa. The weather was usually cold, wet and stormy for days, and sometimes weeks, on end. These outside conditions confined us to the house where boredom, bad tempers and squabbling occurred often. We sorely missed playing with our friends in the park.

To help us better cope with winter weather, Mum would dress us warmly and take us to the indoor botanical garden in Cape Town. She sometimes packed a large sandwich lunch and some fruit. She would hold our hands and walk us up from the railway station. Under umbrellas in the driving rain, we would make our way over muddy paths and puddles to the greenhouse. We would shed our raincoats, close our umbrellas, open the glass doors and enter a warm, protected environment. Once inside, the beauty of orchids and the fragrance of exotic blooms surrounded us. Here we would play happily for hours, despite the gales raging beyond the walls.

Likewise, each day during my prayer time I imagine myself taking the hand of Jesus, shedding my worldly 'rain-gear' and prayerfully opening the doors to the Lord's botanical garden. I enter Christ's protecting presence and feel secure, despite the storms of life beyond the walls.

Prayer: *Dear God, please remind us to make your presence our only port of refuge in any storm. In Jesus' name we pray. Amen*

Thought for the day: When we pray, God offers us a shelter from life's storms.

Keith Honeyman (Western Cape, South Africa)

Always Bearing Fruit

Read Psalm 92:12–15

Go and bear fruit—fruit that will last. Then the Father will give you whatever you ask in my name. This is my command: Love each other.
John 15:16–17 (NIV)

As my husband and I rode along the Adriatic coast, our guide pointed out an island called Brijuni. She told us about an olive tree on this island that is around 1700 years old and still producing olives each year. This tree has endured centuries of drought and war and yet continues to bear fruit. It probably has seeded many new generations of olive trees now producing their own bounty.

Hearing about this tree has caused me to consider the fruit I am bearing and the seeds I am sowing. Have I stood firm during stormy and troubled times, patiently and bravely bearing fruit, not worrying about what lies ahead? In today's quoted verse, Jesus tells us that we have been chosen to bear 'fruit that will last'.

Long after our time of planting seeds and bearing fruit has passed, the fruit of our life's work will continue to contribute to the bounty of love, wisdom, peace and joy that is the kingdom of heaven. All these will start from the simple yet faithful contributions we make today, here and now, to reflect the love and care of God.

Prayer: *Dear God, help us to trust you as we bear the fruit of your love in the lives of others. In Jesus' name we pray. Amen*

Thought for the day: God helps us to bear fruit that will last.

Anne N. Cremons (Minnesota, US)

Small Group Questions

Wednesday 1 May

1. When have you felt God calling you in a new direction? How did you experience this call? Who helped you to recognise God's call?

2. When you have changed direction in your life, have you been excited about the change or fearful? Who or what helped you during this change? What did you learn about yourself by changing direction?

3. In the story of Zacchaeus, which character do you most identify with? Zacchaeus? The disciples? The crowd? How are you like or unlike Zacchaeus?

4. Zacchaeus changes the way he deals with people by giving half of his possessions to the poor. Would you ever consider giving half of your possessions to the poor? How difficult would such an action be? How would giving away half of your possessions change your life?

5. Stephane reminds us that family members, friends, pastors and even strangers can call us to new directions. Have you ever called someone in a new direction? How did you do it? How did that person receive you?

6. How have you acted out your new life in Christ? What actions have you taken to follow God's call?

Wednesday 8 May

1. Have you ever experienced surgery or a serious illness? If so, describe the process of recovery. What was difficult about your recovery? What helped you to recover? If not, what have you heard about recovering from surgery?

2. What kind of spiritual exercises do you do? Do you have a daily spiritual practice? What kinds of spiritual practice are most meaningful to you?

3. Who has been a good example of spiritual health for you? What do you admire about their spiritual health? How do they stay in shape spiritually?

4. On a spiritual health scale, with 1 being unhealthy and 10 being fully flourishing, where would you place yourself today, and why?

5. What new spiritual practice would you like to try? Why?

6. How does your church encourage spiritual health? What programmes, study groups, fellowship or worship practices help you to feel spiritually healthy?

Wednesday 15 May

1. If it had been you in the situation Lissa describes, would you have changed your plans to help the family? Why or why not?

2. When have you felt that being a Christian was inconvenient? Why?

3. What does 'take up your cross and follow Jesus' mean to you? What does following Jesus look like in daily life?

4. Have you ever volunteered at a local food bank or similar ministry? If so, describe your experience. What surprised you? What did you see that gave you hope?

5. How does the thought for the day challenge you?

6. When is it appropriate to say 'no' to someone's request for help?

Wednesday 22 May

1. Which of the people described in this meditation do you feel closest to? Why?

2. Think back to a time when you felt unable to connect with God. What did you do? How did you reconnect with him?

3. Read aloud Psalm 13. Have you ever felt the way the psalmist feels? How does the psalmist cope with feeling abandoned by God?

4. How do you feel about the mystery of God? Are you thankful that God is mysterious? Why or why not?

5. How does your church community support you in times of unbelief? In what way has your church been most helpful during these times?

6. Doubt does not always equal a lack of faith. When have your questions or doubts led you to a deeper understanding of God?

7. How would you encourage someone who is struggling with unbelief or who feels disconnected from God?

Wednesday 29 May

1. Recall a time you visited a place that had changed drastically since your previous visit. How did the changes make you feel? Did you feel disoriented or lost?

2. Is change something you look forward to with excitement or with anxiety? Why?

3. Describe a time of great change in your life. What fixed points helped you to navigate the changes?

4. How does the Bible help you to remain focused even while experiencing changes in your life? What Bible passages comfort you during times of change?

5. Colette describes the 21st century as a time when boundaries are shifting and morality is often unclear. How do you experience life in the 21st century? Do you agree with Colette? Why or why not?

6. How does your faith in Christ help you to deal with the fast-paced changes of the world today? How do you live out your faith in the 21st century?

Wednesday 5 June

1. What do you know about the conflict in Northern Ireland? Did Mary's description of Belfast in the 1990s surprise you?

2. Have you or your family experienced the kind of fear and violence described in the meditation? If so, how did this experience make you feel? How did you cope with the situation? If not, how do stories of violence in other countries affect you?

3. Does your church work with other churches or faith groups in your community? If so, what missions or projects do the groups support? If not, discuss some ways your church could join with another church to help your community.

4. When have you had a conversation with someone of a different denomination or faith? What was the conversation about? What did you learn from that conversation? What did you have in common with the person?

5. When you pray for peace, for what countries, people or issues do you pray?

6. How do you see God working for peace and understanding in your family? In your church? In your community? In the world?

7. What Bible passages give you hope when peace seems impossible?

Wednesday 12 June

1. What is the most adventurous activity you have ever done? What made you want to try it? How did you feel once the experience was over?

2. Think back to a time you were surprised or frightened by the weather and describe the experience. Whom did you turn to for comfort? What did you do to pass the time?

3. What storms are affecting your life currently? What spiritual practices help you to remember that God is present during this time?

4. When you face challenges in your life, what helps you keep going? Who encourages you?

5. Read aloud Mark 4:35–41. How is the disciples' fear similar to or different from your own? Do Jesus' words sound comforting? Why or why not? How do you think you would feel if you saw Jesus calm a storm?

6. For you, what does it mean that God is our rock and refuge? How has God been a refuge for you?

Wednesday 19 June

1. Have you ever had a neighbour who was generous to you? Describe that person's acts of generosity. How did those acts of generosity make you feel?

2. When has someone's generosity inspired you to be generous?

3. Who do you know who uses God's gifts fully?

4. What spiritual gifts has God given you? Which of your gifts have others recognised?

5. What spiritual gifts do you most admire in other people? Why?

6. Read aloud Mark 14:3–9. Was the woman's act generous? Was it too generous?

7. How do you recognise a gift from God? Who helps you to see God's gifts in your daily life? How does reading the Bible, worshipping, or praying help you to recognise and use God's gifts?

Wednesday 26 June

1. How can you relate to Hannah's story? What misery and trouble have you experienced in your life?

2. Do you pray in public? Why or why not? How do others react to your public prayers? What concerns you about praying in public?

3. How do you prefer to pour out your thoughts and troubles to God? In prayer? In song? In poetry? What other methods might you use to communicate your worries to God?

4. When have you encountered someone in despair? Did their despair make you uncomfortable? Why or why not? How did you try to comfort them?

5. When have you experienced God pouring love into your life? Describe the experience. Did you experience God's love through another person? A Bible verse? Something else?

6. How do you rest? What places, practices or people help you to rest? What does it mean to you to find rest in God?

Wednesday 3 July

1. Who taught you to pray? What times of day did that person suggest that you pray? What were you taught to pray for?

2. Have you ever been a member of a prayer group? If so, what about that experience was helpful or challenging to your faith? If not, why not?

3. What does it mean to you to 'pray continually'? How do you try to do this in your daily life?

4. Which of Carol's suggestions seem an especially good fit for you? Are there any of her suggestions you would not do? Should we try to do all of them? Are there any she didn't mention?

5. Which seems easier or more natural to you—speaking to God or listening to him?

6. If you were to 'pray continually' today, what or who would you pray for?

7. What typically prompts you to pray? Thankfulness? Fear? Celebration? Pity?

8. How might your praying continuously impact other people (for instance being observed when you pray before meals in a restaurant)?

Wednesday 10 July

1. What does the question, 'What would Jesus do?' mean to you? How does this question shape the way you respond to others in your daily life?

2. What is the difference between 'being nice' and 'being like Christ'?

3. Where in the Bible do you see evidence of Jesus being bold or courageous? How do those stories of Jesus affect the way you understand him?

4. When have you been bold or courageous in sharing your faith? How was your boldness received? How would you encourage others to be bold as they follow Christ?

5. Is it easier for you to stand up for Christ in a non-church setting or to confront another believer (the way Paul did as recorded in Galatians 2:7–14)? Why do you think this is so?

6. How do you reconcile Ephesians 4:15 with Matthew 5:39? How do you define 'speaking the truth in love'?

7. Describe a time when you 'spoke the truth in love' to someone. Were you able to be Christ-like in your approach? What was the outcome?

Wednesday 17 July

1. Name some people who have helped you in your spiritual formation. How did these people help to shape your spiritual life? What do you admire about them?

2. Thinking back over your own faith journey, how might others who follow after you describe your 'footprints' of Christian discipleship? What 'footprints' would you like to leave for the next generation? How are you working to create these 'footprints'?

3. In Hebrews 12:2, Jesus is described as 'the pioneer and perfecter of our faith' (NRSV). How do you follow in Jesus' footsteps? Which of Jesus' teachings do you find easy to follow? Which teachings are difficult?

4. Whose names come to mind when you hear the phrase 'pioneers of faith'? Why?

5. Read aloud Titus 2:1–8. Does your church formally encourage members to mentor others? If so, describe this programme. If not, do you think it would be good to do so? Would you consider starting such a ministry? Why or why not?

6. Describe one or two of your Christian mentors. Did you choose them for this role or did they initially choose you? What qualifies them to be your mentor? Should we consciously seek spiritual mentors?

7. Do you think it is better to emulate famous strangers or people we know personally? Why? What are good reasons for looking to people as examples?

Wednesday 24 July

1. Describe a situation or period when you felt 'left out'. How did it feel? How did/do you react? How did this situation change for better or worse? How did your faith help you to deal with that situation? What did you learn from this experience?

2. Recall a time in your life when God brought good out of a bad situation. Were you able to recognise the good things God was doing in the moment, or was it sometime much later? Who or what helped you to see or feel God's presence during that time?

3. Read Psalm 22:1–11. How does the psalmist deal with the feeling of being left out and forgotten by God? How are the emotions expressed by the psalmist similar to or different from your own experience?

4. Why might the meditation writer consider the twelve disciples to be closer followers of Jesus than the women who came to his tomb?

5. Does your congregation make visitors feel welcome and new members included? If so, how? If not, what can your congregation do?

6. Who within your community of faith might feel 'left out'? How about in your family, among your colleagues, or in your community? How might you minister to them?

Wednesday 31 July

1. What other lines of 'folk wisdom' can you recall about how we manage our possessions? How do these sayings align with biblical wisdom about possessions?

2. What are some other Bible passages that come to mind that speak about personal possessions or material wealth? Do you find these lessons to be helpful in your own life?

3. What do you think makes us truly rich? Why?

4. In your experience, whose view of giving is more prevalent, the mother in today's meditation or Zacchaeus'? Which way do you lean? How do you respond when someone tells you that giving will make you rich?

5. Describe a time when you were a joyful giver. What made that experience joyful? How was your gift received?

6. How does your church encourage generous giving? How have you given generously in your church or in your community this year? What gifts do you have that you could share with the people around you?

7. Read aloud Malachi 3:10. What do you think God means by this statement? Have you ever put God to the test in this? In other words, do you tithe? Why or why not? If you do tithe, what was the result?

Wednesday 7 August

1. When you are in need of consolation, what scripture passages comfort you? Besides scripture, what other sources of consolation do you rely on?

2. Read aloud 2 Corinthians 1:4. Have you ever noticed this dynamic in your life? When have you had opportunities to help others who are struggling with trials that you have struggled with in the past? How did that feel?

3. When have you been comforted by a friend? How did they comfort you? Did they share words from scripture? Spend time listening to you? Bring you a meal?

4. In what ways does your church community provide comfort to those who are grieving or suffering? Can you think of ways this comfort could be more accessible? What are some new or different ways Christian communities could console one another as a way of sharing God's love?

5. How does God comfort us? Describe a time when you have felt consoled by God. How did that consolation come to you?

6. How could 'our pain… be a gift'? Have you experienced this? When?

Wednesday 14 August

1. Do you experience God's presence daily? If so, how do you experience him? What places or people remind you of his presence?

2. Describe a time when you felt surrounded by God's presence. Where were you? Who else was present? What were you doing? How did you know God was there?

3. What activities or spiritual disciplines help you to become more aware of God's presence in your life? What spiritual practice would you like to try in order to experience him more fully?

4. Have you ever been a sign of God's presence in someone else's life? If so, how? If not, how might you become that sign in the future?

5. Do you think it's more up to us or up to God in order for us to experience relationship with him daily? What prevents people from experiencing his presence?

6. When do you tend to experience God's presence the most? While you pray? When you are in a nature setting? When you are fearful? How does sensing God's presence make a difference for you?

7. How do you sense God's presence in worship at church? Does worship provide tangible signs of his presence? Which ones speak most clearly to you?

Wednesday 21 August

1. Today's author describes feeling uncertain as she moved to another country. When have you experienced this kind of transition or uncertainty? How was God present to you during that time?

2. Jeremiah 29:11 says, "'For I know the plans I have for you,' declares the Lord, "plans to prosper you and not to harm you, plans to give you hope and a future"' (NIV). Have you experienced the truth of these words in your life? If so, give an example.

3. Do you have a clear sense of God's purpose for your life? If so, what is it? If not, how can you search for that purpose? What passages from the Bible offer instruction or direction about discerning God's plan and purpose for us?

4. Think about some people you are drawn to because of their mature spirit. How do you see God working through those people?

5. What gifts do you see in yourself? How is God encouraging you to use your gifts? Are there places where using your gifts feels natural? Are there times when you feel 'out of place'?

6. When was the last time you earnestly asked God what you should do about a decision or a situation? What was the outcome?

7. What does or what could your local church do to help those who are new to your community to find purpose and place?

Wednesday 28 August

1. Have you ever participated in a mission trip? If so, what was the intended purpose of the trip? Did you find, like today's author, that you received just as much as you gave? What did you learn from the experience?

2. Sometimes we tend to think our own culture is somehow better than the cultures in other places. Have you found yourself thinking that at times? Have you had experiences that have changed that view? What were they?

3. When have you experienced another culture? What surprised you? What did you learn about God or your faith through that experience?

4. What types of service opportunities do you enjoy? Why? Are there particular mission or service opportunities you would rather not engage in? What are they, and why do you resist them?

5. How many ways can you name in which we show God's love with others? Which of these ways do you practise routinely? Which of these ways are you more likely to avoid or circumvent?

6. How do you find 'purpose' in life? What is your faith community doing to help its members to find their purpose?

7. Once we find purpose in life, what might prevent us from taking the path that leads us to that purpose? What might help us to pursue or continue that path?

8. How is your faith community inward-focused or self-serving? How is it outward-focused or in service of others? Name some ways you think your faith community could be more engaged in serving others.

The Walk to Emmaus

It was a phone call from a friend that started my Walk to Emmaus. He asked me if I would like to go for a walk; there was nothing unusual about that since we often walked together, along with our wives. So I said, 'Yes.'

'But you haven't asked me where we are going,' replied my friend.

'Well, I trust you, but if it makes you happy, where *are* we going?'

'We're going to Emmaus.'

He went on to tell me that this Walk to Emmaus, which wasn't a traditional stroll but a spiritual 'walk', was to take place in Derbyshire! In case you think I'm talking in riddles, let me explain.

The Walk to Emmaus, part of The Upper Room Ministries, is a spiritual renewal programme designed to strengthen the local church through the development of Christian disciples and leaders. It is also the best thing I've ever done—I'll never be able to thank my friend enough for inviting me to take part.

The Walk lasts for three days. There are 15 talks, given by both clergy and lay people, on themes which include God's grace, the disciplines of Christian discipleship, and what it means to be the church. The whole experience is rooted in prayer, with time for daily meditation, worship and Holy Communion. The Emmaus Community, made up of people who have already completed a Walk, supports the three-day event with prayer, service and acts of love and self-giving. The 'Pilgrims', as those who are making the Walk are known, are gathered into small groups which support one another throughout the three days. Everyone who makes the Walk to Emmaus is also encouraged to form or join a Fourth Day Reunion Walk, in which this model is continued afterwards, and where people support each other in whatever ways they can.

The Walks are all single-sex gatherings and are held in a number of retreat centres. For the duration of the Walk, Pilgrims are asked to put aside the world and its concerns, to allow the team to care for and organise their time, and to accept that all their needs will be met. It may be a daunting thought to begin with, but one that people soon get used to. I've heard it described as 72 hours of being loved by God's people, and what better way is there for us to show the love that God has for us than by loving each other on his behalf?

I loved my Walk, and afterwards I encouraged both friends and family to take a Walk for themselves, by telling them about my special experience, and by 'sponsoring' them, that is, praying that they might feel inspired to do the same.

I would be delighted if you wanted to make your own Walk to Emmaus, and I would like to give you the opportunity to learn more about it, to pray and, when you feel it is right for you and in God's good time, to find out more by contacting me. My name is Peter Richardson, and I am the Regional Leader of the Walk to Emmaus and Chrysalis in Europe (Chrysalis is the youth version of the Walk to Emmaus). As well as explaining more about the Walk, I can give you practical details of where the Walks are to be held, and the cost. I can be contacted by email, peterthecolours15@talktalk.net, or by telephone on 01594 839408.

The Walk to Emmaus was a unique experience for me, and I would love you to be a part of it. Why not take a look at Luke 24:13–35, the story of the first Emmaus walk, and then think about making your own?

Peter Richardson

Moments of Grace

Reflections on meeting with God

Joy MacCormick

From desolation to celebration, loneliness to love, *Moments of Grace* offers a wealth of pithy and thought-provoking reflections on themes connecting God, faith and the journey of life. Poetic meditations are linked with questions for further pondering, to help the reader make links between head and heart, between what they believe, what they wrestle with believing and what they experience day by day.

Joy MacCormick has written this book to help people have a closer encounter with God in prayer, especially those who may struggle to find a place in conventional church worship. She says: 'One of my most powerful motivations in ministry has been, and still is, "seeing the lights come on in people's eyes" as they discover new ways of thinking about and relating to the Holy, and the impact this has on their experience of "life in all its fullness".'

ISBN 978 0 85746 224 4   £6.99
To order a copy of this book, please turn to the order form on page 159.

Also available for Kindle.

The Sacred Place of Prayer

The human person created in God's image

Jean Marie Dwyer, OP

Prayer is not a complicated set of methods or exercises, but as simple as living life, being ourselves and bringing God into our daily routine. Because we are all created in God's image, each of us is the privileged and sacred place of prayer.

Drawing on scripture, the desert tradition, great spiritual figures from history and the author's own Dominican tradition, this book explores the various steps we need to take to nurture our life in God. After laying the philosophical, biblical and theological groundwork, Sister Jean Marie Dwyer goes on to offer rich insights into how we find our true self and our place of belonging.

ISBN 978 0 85746 241 1   £7.99
To order a copy of this book, please turn to the order form on page 159.

Bible Reading Resources Pack

Thank you for reading BRF Bible reading notes. BRF has been producing a variety of Bible reading notes for over 90 years, helping people all over the UK and the world connect with the Bible on a personal level every day.

Could you help us find other people who would enjoy our notes?

We produce a Bible Reading Resource Pack for church groups to use to encourage regular Bible reading.

This FREE pack contains:

- Samples of all BRF Bible reading notes.
- Our Resources for Personal Bible Reading catalogue, providing all you need to know about our Bible reading notes.
- A ready-to-use church magazine feature about BRF notes.
- Ready-made sermon and all-age service ideas to help your church into the Bible (ideal for Bible Sunday events).
- And much more!

How to order your FREE pack:

- Visit: www.biblereadingnotes.org.uk/request-a-bible-reading-resources-pack/
- Telephone: 01865 319700
- Post: Complete the form below and post to: Bible Reading Resource Pack, BRF, 15 The Chambers, Vineyard, Abingdon, OX14 3FE

Name...

Address ....

....Postcode..

Telephone ....

Email..

Please send me................................Bible Reading Resources Pack(s).

This pack is produced free of charge for all UK addresses but, if you wish to offer a donation towards our costs, this would be appreciated. If you require a pack to be sent outside of the UK, please contact us for details of postage and packing charges. Tel: +44 1865 319700. Thank you.

BRF is a Registered Charity

Subscriptions

The Upper Room is published in January, May and September.

Individual subscriptions

The subscription rate for orders for 4 or fewer copies includes postage and packing: THE UPPER ROOM annual individual subscription   £14.10

Church subscriptions

Orders for 5 copies or more, sent to ONE address, are post free:
THE UPPER ROOM annual church subscription   £11.10

Please do not send payment with order for a church subscription. We will send an invoice with your first order.

Please note that the annual billing period for church subscriptions runs from 1 May to 30 April.

Copies of the notes may also be obtained from Christian bookshops.

Single copies of *The Upper Room* will cost £3.70. Prices valid until 30 April 2014.

Giant print version

The Upper Room is available in giant print for the visually impaired, from:

Torch Trust for the Blind
Torch House
Torch Way,
Northampton Road
Market Harborough
LE16 9HL

Tel: 01858 438260
www.torchtrust.org

Individual Subscriptions

☐ I would like to take out a subscription myself (complete your name and address details only once)

☐ I would like to give a gift subscription (please complete both name and address sections below)

Your name...

Your address...

....Postcode.....................................

Your telephone number...

Gift subscription name...

Gift subscription address..

....Postcode.....................................

Gift message (20 words max)..

....

Please send *The Upper Room* beginning with the September 2013 / January 2014 / May 2014 issue: (delete as applicable)

THE UPPER ROOM ☐ £14.10

Please complete the payment details below and send, with appropriate payment, to: BRF, 15 The Chambers, Vineyard, Abingdon OX14 3FE

Total enclosed £.......... (cheques should be made payable to 'BRF')

Payment by ☐ cheque ☐ postal order ☐ Visa ☐ Mastercard ☐ Switch

Card no: ⬚⬚⬚⬚⬚⬚⬚⬚⬚⬚⬚⬚⬚⬚⬚⬚⬚⬚⬚⬚⬚⬚

Expires: ⬚⬚⬚⬚   Security code: ⬚⬚⬚

Issue no (Switch): ⬚⬚⬚⬚

Signature (essential if paying by credit/Switch card) ....

☐ Please do not send me further information about BRF publications

☐ Please send me a Bible reading resources pack to encourage Bible reading in my church

BRF is a Registered Charity

Church Subscriptions

☐ Please send me ... copies of *The Upper Room* September 2013 / January 2014 / May 2014 issue (delete as applicable)

Name...

Address ....

.... Postcode...

Telephone ....

Email..

Please send this completed form to:
BRF, 15 The Chambers, Vineyard, Abingdon OX14 3FE

Please do not send payment with this order. We will send an invoice with your first order.

Christian bookshops: All good Christian bookshops stock BRF publications. For your nearest stockist, please contact BRF.

Telephone: The BRF office is open between 09.15 and 17.30. To place your order, telephone 01865 319700; fax 01865 319701.

Web: Visit www.brf.org.uk

☐ Please send me a Bible reading resources pack to encourage Bible reading in my church

BRF is a Registered Charity

ORDERFORM

REF	TITLE	PRICE	QTY	TOTAL
224 4	Moments of Grace	£6.99		
241 1	The Sacred Place of Prayer	£7.99		
088 2	Servant Ministry	£7.99		
242 8	Facing Illness, Finding Peace	£7.99		

POSTAGE AND PACKING CHARGES				
Order value	UK	Europe	Surface	Air Mail
£7.00 & under	£1.25	£3.00	£3.50	£5.50
£7.01–£30.00	£2.25	£5.50	£6.50	£10.00
Over £30.00	FREE	prices on request		

Postage and packing	
Donation	
TOTAL	

Name _____ Account Number _____

Address _____

_____ Postcode _____

Telephone Number_____

Email _____

Payment by: ❑ Cheque ❑ Mastercard ❑ Visa ❑ Postal Order ❑ Maestro

Card no ❑❑❑❑ ❑❑❑❑ ❑❑❑❑ ❑❑❑❑ ❑❑❑

Valid from ❑❑❑❑ Expires ❑❑❑❑ Issue no. ❑❑❑

Security code* ❑❑❑ *Last 3 digits on the reverse of the card.
ESSENTIAL IN ORDER TO PROCESS YOUR ORDER   Shaded boxes for Maestro use only

Signature _____ Date _____

All orders must be accompanied by the appropriate payment.

Please send your completed order form to:
BRF, 15 The Chambers, Vineyard, Abingdon OX14 3FE
Tel. 01865 319700 / Fax. 01865 319701 Email: enquiries@brf.org.uk

❑ Please send me further information about BRF publications.

Available from your local Christian bookshop.   BRF is a Registered Charity

About
brf:

BRF is a registered charity and also a limited company, and has been in existence since 1922. Through all that we do—producing resources, providing training, working face-to-face with adults and children, and via the web—we work to resource individuals and church communities in their Christian discipleship through the Bible, prayer and worship.

Our Barnabas children's team works with primary schools and churches to help children under 11, and the adults who work with them, to explore Christianity creatively and to bring the Bible alive.

To find out more about BRF and its core activities and ministries, visit:

www.brf.org.uk
www.brfonline.org.uk
www.biblereadingnotes.org.uk
www.barnabasinschools.org.uk
www.barnabasinchurches.org.uk
www.faithinhomes.org.uk
www.messychurch.org.uk
www.foundations21.net

If you have any questions about BRF
and our work, please email us at

enquiries@brf.org.uk

enter